Big Boys

Do Cry

CHRIS DUKE

DEDICATION

To my family, extended and household, this book is a 200-page apology for everything I have put you through.

To my Lucy's Blue Day family, I love you; you have changed my life.

To my wife, this book wouldn't exist if you hadn't stood by me through EVERYTHING. Thank you for just being you.

ACKNOWLEDGMENTS

Cover Model: James Phillip

Editor: Lisa Marie Duke

INTRODUCTION

"Look around at how lucky we are to be alive right now."

It was the third week in March 2020 when I was sitting in the 8th row of the Victoria Palace Theatre in London waiting to see "Hamilton" for the first time. I've always loved musical theatre, as a member of the audience and a performer, and knew I was in for an unforgettable experience. Grant, a friend I'd been in many shows with, introduced me to the unique musical style of the score, and I knew that it was a very sought-after performance. The truth is, I lucked out: the theatre had one "unsellable" ticket left and I got a bargain. The lights came up: the performance began; I laughed; I cried; I sat in awe and stood in appreciation at the end. So much so, I ended up getting a pretty big tattoo on my arm celebrating the musical.

This third week in March is a perfect symbol of where my life was at the time: coming from a deprived area of Glasgow; struggling with mental illness; self-harm and self-sabotage, here I was "on tour" -

visiting schools all over the UK - talking about my journey of recovery through the medium of "Lucy's Blue Day" - the children's book I'd written in 2018 - and I'd had this opportunity to go and see one of the best musicals ever written. Life was so busy and awesome.

Two days later, Boris Johnson put the UK into a national lockdown due to Covid-19. My tours, visits, talking about my journey of recovery all came to an immediate stop!

I had been on the go for two years; stopping when my wife would schedule a break, and that was it. I thought what many others thought, "We have so much time now. We can accomplish so much." And we did, to an extent. I sorted out the garden, we redecorated the living room, we attempted to home-school the kids (left that to my wife pretty quickly because I didn't have the patience) and we tried to keep our business running. I then decided to sit down and write this book.

Writing it has been a time of reflection and self-discovery. There are certain situations I could have handled differently. There were moments I thought my parents knew about and didn't. Times when I've undervalued how much my wife does and how hard she works, even editing these books when she's not a professional editor – you should have seen the state of this paragraph before she got to it – and how important it is to appreciate those around you. Although we're living through one of the strangest times in our history, we are living through exactly that, history. 2020 will go down as a time where we realised that status doesn't matter as much as being kind does. A time when valuing our family, friends, neighbours, communities, and human being came above all else, and a time when negativity and hatred were overpowered by empathy, compassion and positivity.

My Hamilton Tattoo

"Look around, at how lucky we are to be alive right now."

1 FAMILY

The East End of Glasgow is known to many as a "rough neighbourhood" with "tough people" at its core. In Scotland, or most areas of Scotland, telling someone you're from the East End of Glasgow it's assumed that you are tough, rough, maybe even part of a gang, and in the 90s-00s you were described in Scotland as "a Ned" (or "Chav"). However, when you actually live in the area, it's completely different. You are part of a community that cares for one another; a society that has each other's backs and understands the troubles that come with being from a deprived area. We lived in Cranhill; a council estate in the East End and some of my happiest memories are all based around that two-bed flat: 1-up/left, in Crowlin Crescent.

My mum was a stay-at-home mum of two. As a kid, I didn't appreciate what a demanding role this was. In my naivety, I thought my dad was the only one who worked hard because he was out all day and was the breadwinner for the family. As an adult, I know better. My mum would cook, clean, do the shopping, get us ready for school, get my dad's stuff ready for work, keep the house, and look after Archie (our budgie). She looked after our home and was a childminder for many of my cousins and kids of surrounding neighbours. She's a grafter - she doesn't stop, nor knows when to stop, and, of course, she's the best mum in the world. There is something that has always stumped me:

her name. She's known as Rachel or Rae depending on her mood. I got lost in Asda once and went to the customer service desk; they made the Tannoy announcement and called for "Rachel". When she came, she

My mum enjoying a game of "Super Mario" while I was at School

said "Rachel" made her sound like a snob. The next time I got lost – also in Asda – I remembered what she'd said and this time, said "Rae". It made her sound common; either way, I couldn't win. Oh, and I should mention that her Macaroni Cheese is better than anything you have ever tasted in your life.

My dad worked - a lot! He's a blacksmith which is a bit like a welder, but he doesn't like to be labelled a welder, so I'm not exactly sure what to call him - except dad. Drive through Glasgow with my dad, and he'll tell you all the different projects he's been a part of putting together: the brown fence at the "Mother's Pride" factory is one, and the big screens at Celtic Park are another. There are loads he's pointed to over the years, but the one that sticks out in my mind is the graffiti he and my mum left when there was fresh cement somewhere, and

5

they wrote their initials, but I can't tell you about that in case they get into trouble! Working isn't the only thing that defined my dad. Yes, he worked seven days a week, but when he was home, he was always doing something with my sister and me and was very present in our lives. There were some days where my dad wasn't at work for one reason or another, and he would pick us up from school. These were memorable days, and we would talk my dad's ear off the whole way home. He's an excellent dad and Grandad, and there will be points throughout this book that you'll see and understand what I mean. He was the man who drummed it into me that "Big Boys Don't Cry" but was also the man who taught me that they do.

My dad is one of the most loving, caring, and best dads you can get. I feel I have to remind you that it was the 90s-00s which was a very different time, and people had very different attitudes to mental ill health; my dad was no exception. He had to learn the same way many other people are, and

My Dad and his babies

he's still further on than millions are now.

You'll hear more about my extended family later, but I want to tell you a little bit about my dad's brother, Johnny. My Uncle Johnny was a man who was small in stature but huge in personality and kindness. He would show me magic tricks (one of which impressed a girl so much she married me), and he would give me 20p every time I saw him. He had a very special nickname for me too: "Christophantiano".

When I was three, a carnival came to Cranhill. It must have looked incredible with Dodgems, Waltzers, Merry-Go-Rounds and all sorts of games at the park. Everything would have looked MASSIVE, and I'd have been so excited to go to "The Shows"!!! My parents took me and my big cousin, Angela, who's ten years older than me. Anything Angela went on I went on and my parents were happy with it. It wasn't until Angela asked if she could take me on the Motorbikes that my mum drew the line; these were fast, petrol-powered motorbikes that had kids speeding around the track like they were racing in a Grand Prix. Angela went on them and mum, and I went to the side to watch. It would have captivated my little three-year-old self. I must have been in awe of these older kids zooming past on these incredible machines designed for children. I held my hand out to high-five them as they whizzed by at the whopping speed of 7mph! I LOVED this! I'd have seen the flashing lights; heard the people talking; felt the music beat in my chest, and without warning, I'd have felt a tug on my arm, and my mum would have got further away from me. The roar of the bikes would have got louder and louder, and the next thing I'd have felt was the cold concrete hit my head: once, twice, three times then, nothing.

I opened my eyes and couldn't focus. I was in the hospital: The Royal first for a day or two then to Yorkhill Sick Kids Hospital. I stayed for a week there, and I didn't speak the whole time. My mum relays the story to me: the doctors and nurses would come in and ask me some questions: what my name was, my age, and where I lived. I didn't answer. I didn't know anyone, and my mum says I must have felt so scared and alone. There were strangers all around me, and two didn't leave my side the whole time. They brought me snacks and drinks, read to me at night and were still there the next morning. It had been a week, and with no recognition of my family, I headed for a brain scan. The man of the two strangers and I waited at the lift, and it pinged open. He said, "Oh look, Christopher, there's your Uncle Johnny." I said, "Oh, Johnny!" and that was me back. I started chatting with everyone because I knew who they were. They must have appeared right in front of my eyes, and I recognised them, finally!

My mum says it was like I just snapped out of whatever state I was in and was back to being myself again. She describes the whole thing as "an experience" and also says it's the first time my little sister (who my mum was pregnant with) kicked and she felt it as she was sitting beside my hospital bed.

My Uncle Johnny, the man who saved my life

It turned out I was dragged onto the track by someone on the motorbikes and hit my head so hard on the concrete it had affected my memory. I couldn't recognise anyone I knew: mum, dad, my aunties, my uncles, no one; until my uncle Johnny walked out of the lift. We are adamant that it was the special bond my uncle Johnny and I had that brought me back. Into my adult years, he always said to me, "Don't forget, Christophantiano: I saved your life."

I never have.

I went to bed pretty well most nights as a kid. I remember being about five years old, and my mum, dad and I watched a film called "Batteries Not Included." I wish I could remember what it was about, but all I remember was that it had a ridiculously feel-good, happy ending; it was one of those happy endings that caused the lump in the throat. You know that feeling that your emotions are just inside your throat and if you open your mouth, they're going to burst out so you do everything you can to keep them inside? That.

After watching it, I'd gone to bed, and my dad came in to say goodnight. He sat on the little white wooden chair beside my bed, and I made that noise you make when you try to swallow your emotions. Naturally, he asked what was wrong?

"Nothing", I whimpered into my pillow.

He asked, "Did you enjoy the film?"

"Aye, it was good, wasn't it?" and without any restraint, the sobs and tears burst out my mouth, and I couldn't stop them.

My dad looked at me a little taken aback. "What's this?" he asked.

"It's the film, dad." I said through sobs, "It was such a happy ending."

"I know, but you don't need to cry about it. Tell you what, why don't you think about how much your daddy loves you and that should cheer you up a bit?"

That was my dad's go-to whenever I was crying. It worked; it stopped me crying. I would swallow my feelings, think about how much my dad loved me and drift off to sleep.

While writing this, I spoke to my mum and asked if she could remember the film and the ending. I told her what I remembered, and she said, "Yes, I remember. Your dad wanted to cry too." If only I'd known that as a child, but every day is a school day.

The last person in my immediate family to introduce you to is my little sister, Jacqueline AKA Jac, Jack, Jackie, and any other shortened version that crops up. Not only was Jac my best friend, but she was my biggest rival too. We bonded from before she was born. I don't remember this, but my parents said that I had an imaginary friend. This friend would have a place set at the dinner table where my mum would give her some food; I'd push her in the swing at the park; and generally, "play" with this girl who just so happened to be called Jacqueline.

When we were kids, we acted like any brother and sister. We played as best friends one minute and be mortal enemies the next. I'd bring my wrestling action figures into her Barbie World, and we'd combine those worlds somehow. We'd make radio shows together; we played church where I was the priest, and Jac was the congregation (I always had to be the one on the stage); we'd argue, fight, name-call, but we'd go to our bunk-beds and say, "goodnight. Love you." She's very creative, and I still remember one of the songs she made up:

My imaginary friend became real

"I'm such a nice girl, nice girl, nice girl
I'm such a nice girl, nice girl today.
And the dinner was hot, and the dinner was cold,
He fell on the floor, and then he hitted himself."

I didn't say it was a masterpiece, but I still remember it.

Now, she's a fantastic mum to 3 brilliant kids, an incredibly supportive little sister and an amazing daughter to our parents. She's always had my back. I'm not, nor have I ever been, one of the "tough guys" and

I've still never been in a fight against someone where we hit each other. If I were threatened, which did happen from time to time, Jac would come to my defence. As she got older, into teenage years, she was hanging out with those who were "known" in the area and would say to me, "Chris, if anyone bothers you, let me know, and I'll get it sorted." That strength and determination as well as support and having my back has never left, and she's one of my most favourite people in the world.

I moved to Germany at twenty-one, and I think it affected Jac more than anyone else. I'll talk a bit more about this as we go on, but I'd told everyone I was going on holiday, although I knew I wasn't planning on coming back, and I think Jac knew this too. I did come back for her 18th birthday, which was a surprise for her. I'd met a girl, and we both came back to the party. My dad picked us up from the airport, and once the party had officially started, we waited a few minutes before walking in. When we did, Jac looked up to see me, dropped everything and ran to me. She gave me the biggest hug she'd ever given me, and I remember seeing her genuinely happy to see me. I was so glad to be there as well, and I knew that I didn't just have a little sister, but I had a best friend for life.

As I said, Jackie is mum to three exceptional children: Jonpaul is the oldest; then Marlie, and then Libbie (our little miracle). The doctors told Jackie she wouldn't be able to have any more children after having her second, Marlie. I don't know the specifics (you'll learn I never find out the specifics about most things unless I need to know) but I know she was heartbroken. Jackie would go to the doctors regularly to find out if there was a way to have another baby, but there wasn't.

After I'd moved to Forfar with my kids and my wife, Jac asked me if I could take her to the hospital in Glasgow – this was a 190-mile round-trip, but it's Jackie, so I did it without hesitation. She was getting more tests done, and I waited in the car while she did. An hour and a half later, she comes out, and I took her home then headed back to Forfar. That day she was getting a specific medication that could help her have a baby, and it worked. Jackie calls me her "good luck charm".

It wasn't a smooth ride with Libbie. She was born at 30 weeks' gestation and weighed less than 2lbs. She was tiny! Erica (my youngest) and Libbie were supposed to be three months apart, but they're eighteen days apart in age. There were a lot of emotions going on with having two babies so close together: one thriving and healthy and another fighting for her life in SCBU. Feelings of fear, guilt, worry and overall concern. Jacqueline has been through so much in her life; it just wasn't fair that she had to go through this too. Eventually, we were allowed to visit Libbie in SCBU, and it was so strange to see all these tiny babies in plastic boxes designed to keep them alive. We all cried that day. Almost three years later, Libbie is taller than Erica, rowdier and smashing life. She has the cheekiest smile with the cutest dimples and the most amazing curly red hair. She's 100% a fighter, just like her mum.

2 SCHOOL

Nowadays, it seems people keep to themselves, but when we were kids, we knew our neighbours. You had Jeanie who lived downstairs. She quite clearly had the patience of a saint with a family of four with two young children living above her. A common phrase in our house was "Jeanie's In!" when Jack and I would get too rambunctious. Jeanie was an older lady, and she always had the time for Jackie and me. Across from Jeanie were the Smiths; another family of four who I thought were so lucky because they had a garden to play in, and in the summer we'd all be out in the paddling pool while my dad threw water balloons from the veranda (or "granda" as I called it). Across the landing from us, we had Mr & Mrs Muir - an older couple who were the best of neighbours. Mrs Muir was one of those people in the community who everyone knew, and if there was an event going on, she knew all about it and was

Mrs Muir was the perfect neighbour

involved in some way or other. At the top of the close was Wilma and her children: Alan and Alison. Alan was the first person to introduce me to professional wrestling on TV. He would loan me videos of these larger-than-life characters like Hulk Hogan, Macho Man and The Undertaker. I saw this as a "real sport" because I was never really into football or anything other typical "boy sport". Directly above us were the Amato family. I don't remember much about them other than one of the kids was called Joe, and we were the same age but went to rival primary schools.

Lamlash and St. Modan's Primary were the two schools in my catchment area, and being the good catholic boy that I am, I went to St Modan's and was very proud to go there. It was a red-bricked, flat-roofed building that had the most pungent whiff of ammonia when you walked in. To this day, whenever I smell ammonia, it takes me right back to primary school. Our headteacher was called Mrs Hunter. She was a tall, thin, scary lady, and from what I know, she wasn't well-liked by a lot of the grown-ups at Cranhill either. The students were scared of her. She'd screech her whistle in the playground, and when she did that, you'd know someone was about to get into BIG trouble! As scary as she seemed, she always had the best interests of the school and the pupils at heart, and that was obvious. She was the first person to ask me, "Are you okay?" when I acted out and not give me into trouble.

My earliest memory of Primary School was walking in on the first day of p1 and not crying. I was so proud of the fact that I was the only person in my class that didn't tear up when my parents left. Mrs Scanlon, my teacher, was a sweet, very kind, lovely and genuine lady. I always felt that I had a personal connection with her because she lived across the street from my Auntie Anna, and she'd be the only teacher that I would see outside of school. It was always a bit weird seeing a teacher outside of school, wasn't it? It always seemed like they just spent all their time at school and any life out with that didn't exist.

Our first ever Christmas show was a dance routine choreographed by Mrs Hunter (the scary headteacher). We all had girls' red tights on, no top and a sparkly top hat. The thirty 4-5-year olds danced on stage to Frank Sinatra's "New York, New York." Before the performance, we were in our dressing room (our classroom), and we were waiting to go on. In the meantime, the students were giving Mrs Scanlon (kind teacher) gifts, and every time she received one, hugged and kissed the student. Christopher Armstrong stepped up to be next in the, aptly named, "Teacher Present Giving Game" with all the bravado and confidence a 5-year-old could muster. He marched over to Mrs Scanlon, proudly passed her gift over and BAM! She planted a kiss on his lips. He smiled, wiped it away and turned round to go back to his seat. It was at that moment I decided that Mrs Scanlon wouldn't be getting a Christmas present from me.

We were first up for the Christmas show, and as we stood behind the curtain feeling nervous and excited, Mrs Hunter came over to speak to

Mrs Hunter hosting the Christmas Concert

us.

"Boys and girls, I hope you are ready to have lots and lots of fun with your performance tonight."

"Oh! She's quite lovely outside of school." I thought.

"Let this be a word of warning. If I see any of you not looking the right way; waving at mum's and dad's, granny's or granda's, or anyone else, I will come onto that stage and drag you off by the ear – do I make myself clear?" Eek!

"Yes, Mrs Hunter. Thank you, Mrs Hunter", we sang in response.

Sinatra blasted over the speakers as the "Jannie" pulled the rope to open the squeaky curtains, and there we were standing in our red girls' tights ready to perform our very elaborate routine of dancing, kicking and spinning. That night I fell in love with performing and knew it wouldn't be the last time I was on the stage.

After the performance, we were buzzing back in our "dressing rooms", getting changed when I heard Mrs Scanlon say, "Christopher Duke, can you come here, please?"

My mood changed instantly! I, sheepishly, walked over to her wondering what I'd done, or who I'd upset – I'd never been in trouble before, but her tone made me think I'd done something wrong. I kept thinking about what it could have been. Had I sworn? Said something mean or hurtful? Had I hurt someone by mistake? No. What I'd done was much, much worse!! She found the gift that I'd, sneakily, placed on her desk just before we left to do our performance. She reached over and grabbed me in for a tight hug (I don't mind a hug) and then, she kissed me! My first kiss from someone out with my immediate family was Mrs Scanlon, my p1 teacher.

Something I always do is tell whoever will listen when my birthday is (September 14th - add it to your calendars!). Mrs Findlay was my p3 teacher, and I'm pretty sure I was her favourite student. I was friendly, polite and tried my best, so most teachers liked me. In p3 I wore a massive birthday badge on top of my grey uniform. I was so excited and so ready to get lots of birthday wishes and gifts from people in my school. No one said anything when I arrived, and by "playtime", still nothing. I didn't want to make a big deal out of it, so I just waited and waited, and no doubt tried to bring my colossal badge to people's attention in a not-so-subtle manner. By lunch, I'd figured the class, and Mrs Findlay had forgotten about me, so spent the remainder of the time feeling a bit sorry for myself and sad. We went to the library in the afternoon to sing hymns with Mr Lebedis; we sat in our usual lines, legs crossed, ready to sing some of our favourites. Mr Lebedis sat at the piano, as usual, and played the first chord of a song I'd never heard him play before.

Then, *"Happy Birthday to you!*
Happy Birthday to you!
Happy Birthday, Dear Chrissy!
Happy Birthday to you!"

They hadn't forgotten about me at all! They'd planned to make me THINK they had to surprise me with the song. I was delighted! Mrs Findlay got the whole class to make birthday cards for me and a p7 "delivered" them dressed as a postie. I still have those cards, and the feeling of love and acceptance I felt that day is something I'll never forget.

It wasn't until p4 where I met a teacher who didn't like me called Mr McKernan. Whether it was a clash of personalities or something else I don't know; he just didn't like me, and my mum said the same. His dislike for me affected my behaviour and my grades. I remember a time when the boy's toilets were out of order, so we were asked to use the staff toilets instead. They were right next to Mrs Hunter's office; it was also where the staff left their belongings, and the dinner ladies left crockery. One day I'd gone to the toilet to get away from Mr McKernan and, while washing my hands, I spotted the staff car park out the window, and a thought came to mind. Could I drop something out there without anyone noticing? I then looked about to see what I could chuck out. There were scratchy, green paper towels; a small bar of soap; a pile of crockery in a wicker basket - oooh! My heart began racing. I was a good kid; no one would expect it to be me. I picked up a saucer, felt the cold ceramic against my fingers, and placed it on the window ledge, which was already open. With my index finger, I started to push it closer and closer to the edge.

Dare I do this? What would happen if I got caught? It started to wobble. I paused. Then I pushed it. The next few seconds were a sudden rush of regret as the saucer tumbled the three floors to the concrete below, and for some reason, I put my hands over my ears so I wouldn't hear it. Maybe I thought if I didn't listen to it, it didn't happen? Despite my valiant effort to mute the sound, I heard it. I listened to the ceramic smash off the ground and waited. I waited for a few minutes to see if people would come to find out where the noise had come from. There were no alarms; no rush of people to see what happened – nothing happened. I slowly opened the bathroom door to see an empty corridor. I breathed a sigh of relief; no one saw a thing. I continued to throw one item of crockery out the window on every visit to the toilet: a cup here, a saucer there. If it smashed, it went out, and every time I covered my ears to block out the reality of what I was doing.

It had been a few days since I'd been to the toilet in question when Mrs Hunter came into the dining hall one lunchtime. With a stern, demanding-of-attention blast of her whistle, she grabbed our attention and said, "Boys and girls! I am so disappointed to be saying this to you. From now on, all primary four pupils are BANNED from using the bathroom next to my office. You will use the P1-3 toilets instead." There were a few groans and grumbles. "I'm very aware that these toilets are a lot smaller for our younger pupils, but you should have thought of that before you STOLE Mr Lebedis' gloves!"

My heart sank.

I had taken one of my regular toilet trips to get out of Mr McKernan's a few days before and had noticed something new in the bathroom: a lovely pair of leather gloves. I thought these were ideal because they wouldn't make a sound hitting the ground – the perfect crime!!

Mr Lebedis was terrific! I liked him a lot as a teacher. He was the person who introduced me to the world of music: a passion I still hold. He would visit our

The incomparable Mr Lebedis

school once or twice a week to teach us music, play hymns for our school mass and teach us songs for our mini school shows. He taught me the recorder, and I loved it when he played the piano whilst we sang "This is the Day that the Lord has Made" and "All Over the

World". You couldn't help but be mesmerised by his playing and how much fun he was having as he danced and swayed to the music.

How could I have done this to Mr Lebedis? How could I fix it? I took comfort in the knowledge that somebody didn't steal them; a ridiculous attempt to appease my guilt.

Of course, I'd have my recorder lesson that day, and as I walked in and saw Mr Lebedis, my 7-year-old body filled with guilt. I could feel something bubbling inside me, desperate to burst out, and I couldn't hold it in anymore. "WHAT IF THEY WEREN'T STOLEN?" The words erupted from my mouth like a volcano. Mr Lebedis looked at me. "I mean your gloves. What if they just…fell out the window? They might be on the ground in the car park, and I know you get the bus, and won't see them there."

Mr Lebedis didn't say anything. He carried on with my lesson, as usual. The next time he came to school, the leather gloves were covering his hands. I felt such relief! He'd found them, and I'd got away with it. Now, let me make something clear: as an adult, there isn't a doubt in my mind that Mr Lebedis knew what happened when he went to that car park and found his gloves lying on the ground. I also know they would have been pricey. I know when my kids try to do something similar, I can always tell.

I wasn't bullied or popular throughout the school; I was somewhere in the middle. In primary 6 and 7, being well-liked by many was the most important thing to me, and I did everything I could to join in with the "cool kids". There was a prank they used to do where you'd put a drawing pin on the chair of someone who'd stood up, and hoped they'd prick themselves. The fact it was on the bum was hysterical to 10 and 11-year-olds. I have a habit of taking things too far, and one day when walking to school, during the peak of the prank, where I came across a rusty nail. I thought this was excellent! I hadn't seen anyone do one as big as this; it would be the best prank of the lot! I took it with me and was so excited to use it. In Mrs Antoniou's p6 class, Lindsay McLean stood up to get something from the teacher. Now is my chance!! I put the nail on her seat and sat back down, as fast as possible. There it stood, rusty and about 6 inches long, ready to prick Lindsay on the bum. I couldn't retain my excitement; I told Stephen Garrity, my best friend. I just knew I was going to be King of the Class.

"Psst! Look what I just did."

I motioned my eyes to the nail on Lindsay's chair, expecting Stephen to find it hilarious. He gave a little giggle, but I knew he'd go from giggling to laughing hysterically as soon as she sat down. I turned back to look at the nail. Out of nowhere, Lindsay came rushing over and looked at her seat to see this rusted, 6-inch nail sticking right up. She was furious! She grabbed the piece of metal and took it straight up to Mrs Antoniou, and I slinked down in my chair, hoping she wouldn't see me. Stephen had got up while I wasn't looking to tell Lindsay what

I'd done. I thought he was my friend, but even he knew I'd gone too far. Despite my best efforts, the teacher did see me and, of course, she didn't just tell me off, she yelled at me; it echoed through the whole school. It was at that moment I also realised I'd taken it too far, and I learned that one wrong decision like that could change everything – I was now the most hated boy in class, even the boy everyone picked on, Robert Corner, was hating me. Mrs Hunter came into the room (I can't remember if someone had called her in or she heard the teacher, but neither would surprise me). She took me to her office and called my mum. I wasn't allowed to stay in the school for the rest of the day, which was weird because I'd never really been in trouble before. The teachers shouting at me, being sent home, and being hit on the side of my head by my parents wasn't the worst part of that day; I had no friends. All I wanted was to be accepted by the "cool kids", but, once again, I'd gone too far and ruined everything.

The next day I woke up feeling so sick with worry. What would happen today at school? I had a sore head, and my hands were ice cold – this was the first time I remember ever having symptoms like this. I told my mum, but understandably, she thought I was faking it because I was too scared to go into school. As a parent, I'd have felt the same. I put my uniform on, brushed my hair and my teeth and headed out the door. I'd typically walk to school on my own, but that morning my mum came with me because she didn't want me picking up any rusty nails. We arrived at the shop at Bell Rock Court (a little community shop where I used to get Irn-Bru bars or a Quenchy cup) which was just before the school. I stopped and looked at my mum, tears filling my eyes and begged her, "Please, mum. I don't feel well. I can't go to school today." Her reply was something along the lines of a couple of words beginning and ending with "F", and she turned to go home without me. I reluctantly headed towards the gate, and before I got into the school grounds, I threw up, all over my newly polished school shoes. The janitor spotted what had happened, took me to Mrs Hunter's office, and within the hour, I was back home.

Looking back, this is the first time I recall my mental health affecting my physical health. We didn't have a term for "mental health" then, but I did realise I felt the way I did due to what I was feeling inside my mind. My hands go blue when I have extreme emotions or anxiety, so my mum and my wife know when something is wrong.

I was off for a week with this "mystery illness". The doctor said it was a viral infection and gave Calpol to help me through it. A week to a 12-year-old was a long time; long enough for things to go back to normal. I was at school the following Monday, and everything had resumed: the popular kids were still popular, and I was in the middle of the pecking order. One thing did change; no one was bullying Robert Corner anymore. It seemed all he needed was a common enemy, and he was part of the class. At least something good came from my prank-gone-wrong.

I appreciate I'm not coming across very well with these stories; some may even call me "a little arsehole" and you'd be right. I don't know why I needed that acceptance so much, or why I wanted to fit in – I suppose a lot of it is humans just want to be liked and accepted, but it got a little desperate at times.

Other than the incident with the nail, and the aftermath, I did have friends throughout primary school. Patrick McLaughlin was my best friend from p2. I'd go to his house after school, have dinner with his family and watch his TV. He had SKY TV, and I thought this was fantastic! We used to watch The Simpsons, football (although I was never really interested in that) and wrestling. What I didn't realise was that he didn't have SKY. It was the man who lived across the street; somehow, Patrick's TV picked up whatever that man was watching on Channel 5. If he was watching The Simpsons, so was Patrick; if he was watching football, so was Patrick; and if he was watching wrestling, so was Patrick (and me). He wasn't allowed to watch Channel 5 after 10 pm though.

Stephen Garrity was my friend from primary 4. Mr McKernan (the teacher that didn't like me) didn't seem to like Stephen either, so this bonded us. Stephen was hilarious. He was the class clown. He'd spend most of the time making me laugh; make jokes all day; make others laugh and, somehow, never got caught by the teacher. Our friendship was different from Patrick's and mine. I never went to Stephen's house, and he never came to mine; we were only friends in school. Stephen telling Lindsay about the rusty nail wasn't the only time he did something behind my back either. In primary 5, there was a new boy in school: Colin Usher. Colin was the first black person to come to our school – East End of Glasgow in the 90s was a predominantly white neighbourhood. Colin was friendly and ended up hanging out with Stephen and me. One day Stephen was doing his usual joke-making antics when he started singing a hymn: "I, the Lord of Sea and Sky. I have heard Colin cry. Ooh-La-La, La-La La-Lee..." and I'm not going to finish it because I'm beyond ashamed of even laughing at it. It was a racist song, and downright horrible, but in my childish need to have friends, I laughed – loudly. So loudly, Kerry Ann Campbell (one of the most popular girls in the school, and my primary school crush) asked why I was laughing. I sang the song to her, and she told the teacher that I was racist to Colin. Mr Kelly looked at me with raised eyebrows, but I was so sure that Stephen would speak up and say, "No, Mr Kelly, it was me." but he didn't. He sat still and let me get into told off on my own (a telling off I deserved), but that's when I started to think that people look out for themselves only.

Those experiences taught me that having friends isn't the be-all and end-all. I decided to keep myself to myself and carry on with my passions. I concentrated on the recorder again with Mr Lebedis – I can still play Three Blind Mice on it as well. I branched out and started learning the piano (I had a keyboard at home and figured out how to play "Happy Birthday" by ear). If someone played something for me, I could play it back; now, I'm not talking Mozart, Beethoven on 'Flight of the Bumblebees' or anything, but it was still pretty cool for a Primary

6 to be able to do that. I started to realise I was far brighter than I gave myself credit for. My grades started to get better, and by the end of p7, I was at the top of my class in maths, English and music. Something else came from this "head down" attitude I'd adopted; I started to attract people to me. People started wanted to be my friend; they liked who I was and respected me.

And then we all went to secondary school to start all over again.

3 EDUCATION

Trigger Warning and disclaimer – this chapter discusses self-harm in detail

I started secondary school as a bit of a "celebrity" due to an incident that happened over the Summer Holidays. August 1995, I will never forget. At this point, we lived in a different flat in Cranhill: three bedrooms, one-up, in a T-close. To this day, I still have no idea what T-close means, but it's still there. The tenements we lived in were being renovated and were being "done up" by the council. We had some lovely double-glazed windows installed; posh, new chip stones on the outside of the close; fresh paint; new verandas, etc. It was going to make the scheme looks so much better. As the buildings were four-storeys high, the council had to put scaffolding all around every structure in our area, which we called "The Triangle". We would see workers on the frame drilling, sawing, hammering and making our homes look a million times better.

On a Wednesday in the middle of August, Jacqueline and I had gone to the entrance door to wait for Christine - our cousin – who was taking us swimming. We stayed just outside the door, which had a canopy above it as a shelter. About 3-feet from this canopy was the scaffolding. Jacqueline, eight years old, decided to start swinging round, and round, and round on the bar that was holding up the canopy. I wasn't watching her; I was standing in a world of my own. The next thing I see is Jac running towards me with a hole, smack bang in the middle of her forehead, and blood trickling down her face. She was crying hysterically and couldn't speak. Feeling guilty because I hadn't been keeping an eye on her, I took her upstairs to my mum and dad. They took one look at her and thought someone had shot her in the head. I suppose when you have kids, you always imagine the worst thing possible, even though it doesn't make sense. After a couple of minutes, she started to calm down and said to my dad that she had been "electrocuted".

"Nah," we all thought to ourselves "she's probably just being overdramatic".

My dad eventually asked me to show him what happened. (I didn't know; remember I wasn't watching her.) All I knew was that she was swinging on the pole that held up the canopy. We went to the bottom of the close, I stood next to the bar that held up the roof, and I said to my dad, "She just touched these two poles here." And I grabbed them.

A sudden tension surged through my body. It felt like a giant blood-pressure machine was wrapped around me and was squeezing! Everything was blurry, and it felt like my head was sinking and to my neck. I could see the outline of my T-shirt, which only reinforced the thought. I could hear a loud "hum" and feel a buzzing rattle run through me from head to toe. I felt my eyes rolled into the back of my head, and the next thing I knew, I'm sat on the ground outside of my close.

Silence.

My dad tells this story a little differently:

Jaqueline had come upstairs saying that she'd had an electric shock off the scaffolding, and I asked Christopher to go downstairs with me and show me what happened. He grabbed the two poles and became stuck fast to the scaffolding. In my line of work, I've seen this sort of thing before, and I knew that I couldn't grab him because if I did, I also would have been stuck. I looked around for some wood; couldn't see anything at all. I looked down at my feet and realised I had rubber gorilla slippers on, and I lifted my leg, and I kicked my 12-year-old son as hard as I could. He fell to the ground, silent.

For about 10-15 seconds, I sat in complete silence, not knowing what happened; not knowing what was going on; not even knowing if I was alive. I started crying and ran upstairs to the house. I don't remember much about what happened next. I do know that, within half an hour,

31

my extended family filled my house - most notably, my Granny and Granda Duke. We always visited them, never them us, so it had to be something big going on. I remember Jac and I spent the night in the hospital. When the doctor tried to take my blood pressure, I panicked, because it felt like it was happening again.

The next day we were all over the newspapers. Scotland Today came to the house; took videos of the close and the scaffolding, and journalists interviewed my dad for various news articles on radio and newspaper. We were on the front page of the Daily Record, and my dad's "claim to fame" is that he was on page 7 of The Sun.

When we were being checked out by the doctor the next day, Scotland Today came on the TV, and we were the headline news. My mum turned to the doctor and said,

My claim to "fame"

"Well, that's it, we won't win the lottery now."

The doctor turned to my mum with a stern look and a gruff voice and said, "No, Mrs Duke. You HAVE won the lottery."

The "celebrity" status lasted for that first day of school. Nothing particularly "interesting" happened those first few years. Mr Malone (headteacher) send me home to change, once, because my shirt was blue instead of white. That was it until late into the second year where I went into the music room and started playing the piano. All my previous "accolades" from my piano playing were one-handed, but whatever happened on this day, something clicked, and I could play the base-notes with my left, the chords with my right and starting "vamping" some oom-pah style tune. My class stopped and looked at me in shock. Mr McLean stopped and looked at me in surprise. I stopped and looked at my hands in amazement; what I was playing worked! At that moment I knew, I wanted to make music.

The Music Department at St. Andrew's Secondary was a wonderful place. We weren't just teachers and students; we were a family. Music became my escape, and playing the piano was my way of relaxing or unwinding when things were getting stressful. I enjoyed Music so much that I asked my mum if she'd use my varicose veins as an excuse not to do PE anymore, and she agreed – she also has varicose veins, so understood that it wasn't conducive to PE.

Des McLean (we called him Des when the other teachers weren't about because he treated us like his peers) is a great human being. He's who my mum called when I had my first bout of depression in 4th year. She knew how much I respected him, and he'd be able to find out if there was something needing attention. On my way up to Music, when the rest of my class were at PE, he said to me, "Chris, come into my class for a minute, will you?" I walked in to find Mr McLean, Mr

McKenna and Mrs Smith. I thought I was getting into trouble for something. He calmly said, "Are you okay, Chris? Is there anything wrong, or anyone bothering you? Do you have a "little Chris" running about somewhere that we don't know about?" He giggled, nervously, at that one. We spoke for about an hour; not about anything in particular, but just chatted. I should also mention there was no "little Chris" running about either! This conversation was a relief, but it got me worrying that more people were concerned about me.

Another teacher who changed my life was Mr Gordon. He came to our school as a substitute for music, initially. He was this tall, handsome, long-haired fellow whose talent on the piano was incredible! He encouraged our class to audition for Glasgow Schools Youth Theatre's adaptation of The Little Shop of Horrors – he was a freelance music teacher, so worked in many different musical capacities. I'd auditioned for the role of Seymour, and it appeared I wasn't as good an actor as I thought I was. I didn't get any part and felt very disappointed. Iain said to me he was disappointed as well, as he was sure I'd get the role, but I just didn't do a good enough job. I stayed in the chorus and got to know Iain and his way of working a lot better. He ended up coming to our school full-time a few months later, so it was nice to know the new teacher already. Iain knew when you weren't putting 100% into your work. He'd say, "Get your finger out your arse and get that fucking work done!" Harsh, but it worked!

I'm a bit of a geek – something I've learned to embrace over the years, and something my wife loves about me. Here's a couple of stories that made me cringe a little when reciting:

I asked Iain to help me audition for Stars in their Eyes – a TV show, hosted by Matthew Kelly, where people dressed up as their hero and impersonated them on national TV. I didn't have the backing track, so I asked Iain to play it on the piano while I sang. Elvis Presley was my absolute favourite (and probably still is); I wanted to sing "Jailhouse Rock". I expected him to practice a bit, but he just sat at the piano and played the WHOLE song, WITHOUT the music – even the solos!!! I knew I wanted to be just like Iain Gordon! He was amazing! I didn't get through to the audition in the end.

Second "geek story" is that I wanted to be like Iain Gordon so much I started dressing like him, while on work experience - at my school. Iain wore a tie to match his shirt, so I'd do the same. I'd use my wages from being a busser at Frankie and Benny's to buy new shirt-and-tie combos. He'd shaved his beard into a goatee and had cut his long hair, and you guessed it, I did the same. I know it sounds ridiculous and very "cringe", but I admired him.

Iain mentored me when I auditioned for university. An institute full of accomplished musicians who were better than me. I'd come as a big fish in a small pond to small fish in a sea of talent! I felt so intimidated and eventually dropped out through my lack of commitment to improve. If I didn't master it right away, I gave up.

I didn't spend all of my time in the music department though, during my latter years in school I started to hang around the English department too. I bonded quite a lot with a new teacher there called Lesley McErlane. St. Andrew's was her first posting fresh out of University and she formed friendships with quite a few of us older students. Lesley loved wrestling, so I was already invested in this friendship. She helped me get the best grades I ever had in English, and we even performed together on stage for the school "Stars in their Eyes" competition.

During the height of my depression at school, I arrived home and emptied my bag to find a letter, it was on Winnie the Pooh paper and was two pages long, front and back. It was from 4 of the English teachers, one of them being Lesley, explaining how worried they were about me and that if I ever needed to chat, they were there for me, not as teachers, but as friends. I was going to be ok.

Lesley continues to help me to this day, even though she lives thousands of miles away from me, she still mentors me in my writing and was the first person to edit Lucy's Blue Day when we were working on that. She is an amazing person and a fantastic friend and the students in Washington DC are very lucky to have her.

My best friend and I met in the Music Department. We don't see each other anywhere near as much as I'd like to, but we had a fantastic relationship in high school. Brian struggled with his mental health for a long time. In 3rd year, he came out to his friends and family. A lot of us suspected that he was gay, but it took a lot for him to be his authentic self, especially in a strict catholic school, but we'll come to that a little later.

The first time I'd ever experienced the death of someone close to me was when I was at school. I was in Mr McLean's music class when the department base phone rang. Miss Smith answered. This time, she came into class, which wasn't normal. My stomach turned. "Chris, can you go down to the office, please? Take your bag and coat, too", said Mr McLean after speaking with Miss Smith.

I took the long walk through the corridor to the head teacher's office. As I approached the Crush Hall (what we called the area between the assembly hall and the dining hall), I saw the deputy head with my little sister, Jackie. Neither of us knew what was going on, or what was about to hit us. We walked into the office to see our mum and dad there; my dad looked down. He couldn't look at us. My mum eventually said, "Your Granny Duke died last night." Jac burst into tears and ran into my dad's arms. I just stood, silently – in shock. My mum came over to hug me and said, "It's okay; you can let it out." I didn't have anything to let out, though.

Fifteen, at high school, and this particular lunchtime I just wanted to go home; it wasn't long after my Granny Duke had died, and I just didn't want to be at school. It wasn't far to home; so, I took the 5-minute walk, and let myself in - I was "a big boy who was old enough to have keys" by then.

The house was empty. I'd never gone home at lunchtime before. I would typically be found in one of the music classrooms after eating, tinkling away on the piano, waiting for the bell telling me lunchtime was over. A strange atmosphere filled the house, almost as though the house knew I wasn't supposed to be there. I didn't know what to do with myself because truth-be-told, I didn't understand why I'd gone home. I found myself just wandering around the house trying to keep myself amused, passing time until I had to take the 5-minute walk back to school.

I found myself sat in my bedroom, looking at the various wrestling posters I had on my wall. I had loads: Bret "The Hitman" Hart, Undertaker, The British Bulldog, but there was one poster that always stood out; it was a picture of Shawn Michaels (The Heartbreak Kid) with blood oozing down his face - a massive oxymoron to the Spice Girls posters I had before the wrestling ones. The wrestling matches and the violence was all predetermined. I knew this. I also knew the technique the wrestlers used to create the bloody image in the poster. It's called "blading" and is achieved by taking a razor blade and dragging it across the forehead, discreetly, during the match, and the blood mixed with sweat creates the illusion of a lot of blood running down the face. I stared at the poster of Shawn Michaels. I couldn't stop gazing at the blood dripping down his face.

I had a sudden urge to recreate this illusion. I, frantically, searched through my dad's things for a razor, and it wasn't long until I found the yellow plastic handle of a single-bladed BIC razor. As I lifted it to my forehead, I could feel my heartbeat faster, pumping the blood through my body; and by the time the cold metal touched my skin, my heart was beating so fast I could hear it. I dragged the razor blade from left to right across a 3-4cm area just above my eyebrow. I could feel the sting of my skin breaking and the metal of the blade making contact with the nerves underneath, but I didn't stop.

I could feel a warm liquid flow down the side of my face: one cut for my Granny dying, another for school stresses, and a third for the worries I had about my friend. The feeling was euphoric. It was releasing every bottled-up emotion I'd felt for a long time. My feelings were pouring down my face in a warm, "crimson mask" hiding me from the outside world. For some reason, I don't know why, but I decided to walk to school with my face covered in blood. I hadn't seen anyone on the way to school, but in school, a 6th-year student saw me and ran straight to the headteacher. Mr Malone was a great headteacher: he cared about every pupil at his school, so when he rushed out to check on me, he had that "parental concerned" look, and it was genuine. He took me to the nurse's office, and they asked me what had happened. I didn't want to tell anyone that I'd cut myself, so I did what I'd got pretty good at and lied. I said I'd fallen and bumped my head. They might have believed me had I not had multiple abrasions across my forehead, so they started coming up with other scenarios. Maybe a cat scratched me while I'd passed out? Or perhaps I'd fallen onto some glass? I just played dumb to everything.

They called my mum to get her to come and get me. I expected this, but I didn't expect my mum to phone my dad. He could always see through my bullshit lies. As soon as I saw my dad sitting in the office, I knew he'd not believe me. He said, "Do you think I'm daft, Christopher? I know what you did, but I don't know why you did it." Neither did I.

I self-harmed once more when I was at Uni studying music. The stress of Uni; moving out of my parents on bad terms; having no money; few friends and general life worries left me with that familiar feeling of needing relief. Please understand that self-harm is not the way to feel relief. There are so many other healthy, safer, more manageable ways to deal with that emotion, and I'll do everything I can to ensure people know that.

The latter years of secondary were my favourite. I'd become a "mainstay" in the Music Department and was one of its star pupils. Music became my life. I was the lead in most of the school productions and was reasonably popular. I was once allowed to be Musical Director of the primary school's production of Joseph and the Amazing Technicolour Dreamcoat and was over-the-moon! I knew all the songs, and I thought I'd be an astounding teacher. Three weeks into the rehearsals, I stopped going. I knew the kids in that primary were waiting on me in the hall, ready to rehearse, but I let them down. It was a fantastic opportunity to work with local kids and to gain experience as a Musical Director, but I squandered the whole thing by getting in my way. I feel this is the starting point on my journey of self-sabotage.

4 RELATIONSHIPS

You know that one friend you can go years without seeing, but as soon as you're in their presence again it's back to how it was the last time you saw them? Well, that's what it's like with Brian. We met during a school production: Jonah and the Whale – Brian played God; I was the whale. We didn't have some deep, emotional connection, but we got on so well by pointing out funny things and making each other laugh. For instance, spotting a piece of fluff on someone's trouser bottom was hilarious to us. One day, Brian's mum gave me a lift home; her name is Mary. I liked Brian, and I wanted his mum to like me. I was talking about how I was born in America, in a little town called Casper, Wyoming. I described how my mum went into early labour on the way back from their holiday in the States, and the plane had to make an emergency landing. My mum and Mary met, and they discussed the subject of my miraculous birth. Of course, my mum told Mary that it was utter crap! I was born in Glasgow at The Royal. I have no idea why I said this BS story to Brian and his mum, but Mary told Brian it was all lies and, of course, he stopped talking to me. Yet another self-sabotage situation for goodness knows what reason. Thankfully, and luckily, Brian forgave me, and we came best friends from second year onwards. We were inseparable: we'd meet at the same spot every day; go to class together, be separated for chatting, and we'd spend most of our time outside of school together. We'd fall out as all teenagers do, but it wouldn't be long before we'd be running back to each other, arms open and in slow motion like the movies.

Brian (left) and me

Brian and I shared a lot of "first". We had our first girlfriends at the same time, and we tried smoking together too. Brian told me that he was gay before telling anyone else, so we've always had a bond. Brian coming out caused a bit of controversy – it was the 90s, and it was a catholic school. In Religious Education, we wrote about a moral issue we felt about, passionately. I wrote about beliefs and the catholic treatment towards those who are gay. I wrote that I had a friend who was gay, that being gay doesn't change the person by nature; we are all God's children. I was delighted with my essay, and I felt I'd defended my friend too. At dinner, my parents said outright, "Do you have something to tell us?" I started wondering if Jac and I had fallen out again, or if I'd broke something, but nothing came to mind. "Chris, are you gay?" My mum asked.

What? Why would they ask me this? I have a girlfriend. What made them ask this?

It wasn't until my dad said, "Why did you write that essay?" How did they know about that? The school don't share work with our parents, do they? Well, it turned out my RE teacher had read my paper and was concerned, so took it to Mr Malone. He was a devout catholic who, as far as I was aware, believed homosexuality was wrong, and he'd told my parents I was confessing that I was gay. Now their questions made sense. I explained what the topic of the essay was, and what I'd chosen to discuss. They were friends with Mary and William (Brian's mum and dad) so knew that Brian was gay. They knew I was trying to defend my friend. I was furious! I wasn't angry because my teachers thought I was gay; I was raging because my headteacher had taken an essay, called my parents and told them I was gay. That's not right. I went into Mr Malone's office the next day to give him a piece of my mind. "How dare you phone my parents and tell them I'm gay which is not true and even if I was, it's my place to tell them, not yours!" He looked dumbfounded, but he apologised and explained that as it's a catholic school, they have to adhere to the catholic education rules. Brian changed a lot of minds at that school, Mr Malone included and I don't think he even realises the impact he had at St Andrew's Secondary School. Brian was the first person to come out at the school in our generation, but he wasn't the last. Brian was the definition of a "best friend". He always encouraged me to believe in myself and to have more confidence. Brian was always telling me to audition for the lead roles in school shows, and if it weren't for all of that, I wouldn't be doing what I'm doing now. He got me to join the Glasgow Schools Youth Choir. He was already a member: a tenor, and I was a base. I was quite handsome at 16 as well, and the choir had a lot of girls in it, so I had no trouble getting a girlfriend. I went out with a girl called Karen for a while, but it didn't work out, and I left the choir after that ended.

I used to bump into people from the choir, and they'd always remember me (I have one of those faces). I am awful at remembering names (if I've forgotten your name, I'm sorry!). It was a few years later when I was working at Frankie's (what those of us who worked there called Frankie and Benny's) when another waiter came up to me and said there was a girl at Table 14

The handsome Frankie & Benny's waiter

asking about me. I went over to see who it was, and there was a girl called Laura, who'd been in the same choir as Brian and me. She was always very quiet, and I hadn't noticed her before. It turned out to be her 18th birthday, so I did what I did for birthdays: I popped a candle in a dessert and got the restaurant to sing "Happy Birthday" to her. Laura had given her number to the waitress serving her to offer it to me as she left. I'm not and have never been, a 3-day-wait kind of guy, so I was straight to my locker, saved her number in my phone and sent her a quick text. I was off the following Saturday, so we scheduled a date. After a week of flirtatious texts back and forth, I took her to

Fatty Arbuckle's (25% discount) and then back to Frankie's for some drinks (free depending who was on the bar). It was that night that Laura and I decided to become boyfriend and girlfriend.

Laura was amazing. She was so pretty, very kind and very, very smart: completely out of my league. I was her first "proper" boyfriend, and I was completely paranoid. I kept thinking she was going to leave me for someone better; someone more suited to her. I admit I ruined our relationship with my jealousy. I was paranoid, possessive, and so scared to lose her that I commented on something she was going to wear on a night out with friends. Her skirt was too short for my liking, and I said, "You're not going out like that, are you?" My mum heard me and went through me. My mum telling me I was out of line should have been my wake-up call.

Here is how I remember our conversations when Laura came back from a night out with friends:

Me: Did you have a good night?
Laura: Yeah.
Me: Did you get drunk?
Laura: A wee bit.
Me: Did you pull?
Laura: No.

I'd tell myself that this is a running joke and then carry on having a normal conversation.

At college one day, I was sitting in the union with the usual pit in my stomach, waiting on Laura's text to let me know she was awake from her night out the night before. I was well acquainted with this feeling by now. My mind continuously ran through thoughts like: What was she doing? Who was with her? What happened last night? The paranoias were in my head because everyone knew nothing would happen.

Then she got in touch:

Me: Did you have a good time?
Laura: Yes.
Me: Did you get drunk?
Laura: A wee bit.
Me: Did you pull?
Laura: Yes.

It was a punch right in the gut! Everything stopped. The world just stopped spinning and came crashing down. Laura had kissed someone the night before. The thought of her kissing someone else just crushed me. It broke my heart. How could she do that to me? I burst into tears and ran for the bus to go home – just like the little piggy that cried all the way home. I told my mum what happened when I got in. I expected some comfort, some "there, there, sons" but I got, "well, do you blame her?" I thought my mum had lost it. She should have taken my side; Laura had cheated on me!! The love of my life had kissed someone else, and I was heartbroken. It took a long time to realise it was me who led her to do it. My constant questioning, paranoia, and jealousy had led to her cheat on me. I didn't physically make her kiss the guy, so that responsibility lies with her, but I drove her away. I spent the following three weeks in bed; a mess. I didn't eat, shower, or look after myself. I cried – a lot! I also left college. I could sit here and blame the relationship ending for leaving college, but to be honest with you, and myself, I wouldn't have passed anyway. If there had been a course on smoking, drinking and skiving, I'd have passed with flying colours.

After college, I started to get more involved in recreational projects. I looked for various drama groups to join, and my uncle Alan asked me if I'd like to join the Newland Concert Brass Band. It had been a while since playing the trombone, but I decided to give it a go anyway; I was sure it would be fun. The Newland Concert Brass Band were a community band based in Bathgate, West Lothian. The members were mainly amateur players and hobbyists. Alan got me a loan of a trombone and picked me up every Monday night to drive me to Bathgate from Cranhill. Everyone in the band was friendly, and I thought they were all fantastic players. So much so that I played quietly so no one would hear my mistakes – I was a bit rusty. The band was twinned with a brass group in Neheim, Germany. We'd visit them, and they'd come to Scotland too. When I joined, it happened to be our turn to go to Germany, and I jumped at the chance to spend a week in a country I'd never been to before. What I wasn't too thrilled about was the 2000-mile bus trip: Bathgate to Dover, across the sea, through France, Amsterdam before arriving in Neheim.

Germany was amazing! We arrived in time for Jäger Fest – a yearly festival to celebrate the best hunters in the region. It was an excuse to

drink lots of beer, eat lots of food and celebrate! It was on this trip that I met Sabrina. A pretty girl, two years younger than me who came along to the band parties as her friend was in one of the bands. I liked this friend, although she didn't speak any English. Sabrina could speak English and German, so she was our translator. As the conversation progressed, it became less of a three-person conversation and started being a two-person conversation. Sabrina

Jäger Fest - Germany

and I hit it off, and we spent the rest of the trip together. I threw myself into the relationship with Sabrina from the start – completely, 100% in – she was the one! When we got on the bus to return home, I cried. I cried most of the way home, and when we arrived back in Scotland, I decided I was moving to Germany. I worked in TGI

Friday's and was making good money for a 20-year-old still living at home. I told everyone I'd be heading off to Germany to see my girlfriend on September 17th (not long after my 21st birthday). When I booked that Ryanair flight, there was no doubt in my mind that it was a one-way booking, and I wasn't coming back.

Living and holidaying in a foreign country are worlds apart. I arrived at a party Sabrina's parents threw for me, which was so lovely. I met her Uncle Klaus, who was so funny; her Oma, the only 95-year-old who could drink Ouzo like it was going out of fashion and the rest of her family. However, when Monday arrived, it was "real-life", and I needed a job. A month into my living there, I started to notice that something seemed off. Sabrina had this friend who'd come over every day, and she'd translate for me as he didn't speak English.

As the visits became more regular, the translations became less, and before I knew it, the three-way conversations became two-way conversations, this time though, I was the one being ignored. There are a few words in German that are very similar to English, so I found I'd spend my time listening out for any comments I recognised. I would hear my name; the words "sex" and "kuss" (German for "kiss"). Sabrina and this guy would disappear to her room for a while and leave me sitting watching MTV and Viva La Bam with German subtitles. There's no doubt in my mind you're reading this and have either slapped your head in your hand thinking 'Chris, Chris, Chris, come on' but I was blinded by "love". I was so desperate for love that this whirlwind holiday romance turned into something ugly and cruel. Sabrina did have a lot of male friends, and it never bothered me because I got on better with women as well; she even had a pen-pal from England called Ben. This one night I was watching MTV in her room, she was on her bed texting on her phone (like she usually did) when my phone lit up and vibrated. I'd got a text, which was unusual because my friends and family couldn't text as it was international rates back then. I picked up my phone, and it was a text from Sabrina. She looked up and said, "Who's that?" in German. I said, "it's from you...?" and she leapt out of bed and tried to grab the phone off me. It read, "I love you, Ben and I can't wait to come over to England to live with you." I didn't say anything to her for the rest of that night. I lay on the cold sofa in her bedroom in silence while she lay on her bed. The next morning, I woke up with a gentle hand on my side, which turned into an affectionate hug. She didn't say anything, but I assumed it was her way of apologising, so I accepted it.

Sabrina and I were out on the town one night when I fancied myself some pizza. There was only one pizza shop in Neheim, and as we got closer, I could feel her get more and more agitated. I kept quiet. I knew if I said the wrong thing she'd just blow up – it happened a lot before, and I didn't want to poke the bear. As we got to the pizza shop, she said, "I don't think we should get pizza. I think we should go home." By this point, I'd started to realise how controlling she was and how stupid I'd been. She wouldn't allow me on MSN to speak to my friends and family; I'd met a friend at work (in Germany) who I wasn't allowed to be friends with because she was a woman, and any money I made went into her bank account which I wasn't allowed to spend. That night was a breaking point. I wanted that pizza!

"No! I'm going in. I really want a pizza." Then she started. First was the name-calling, demeaning and shouting at me in front of everyone around, and then she stormed away in the direction of "home." I'd been in Germany for about six months, so my German was pretty good. I walked into the pizza shop, and the guy said to me, "You're that Scottish guy, right? Sabrina's boyfriend." I said, "Yes I am." and he laugh-scoffed at me. The laugh-scoff either told me she was sleeping with him and he knew about me; he knew about me and didn't like me based on what she'd said, or he knew she was treating me poorly. Whatever it was, this is why she felt more agitated as we got closer to the pizza shop.

I got back with my 12-inch pepperoni pizza to find Sabrina packing my bag – something she'd done before to keep me in line. She knew I had nowhere to go, so I had no choice but to plead with her to stay, but not this time. I wanted to go; I was happy she was packing my bag. After a heated argument, I took my packed suitcase and started to walk out of the room. As I stepped over the threshold, I felt a sharp tug on my neck. Sabrina had grabbed the neck of my good jumper and pulled me back into the room – jarring my neck in the process. She started slapping me, and then she started punching me. I had my arms up protecting my head, and all I remember thinking was my dad saying never to hit a woman, but to defend myself. All I could think was if I hit her, is it self-defence, or is it hitting a woman? I don't know how it stopped, but when it did, I fell asleep on the couch in her room and she in her bed; like usual. The next morning was that familiar gentle hand on my waist, but I knew it would be the last.

I stayed for a few more weeks and used the upcoming Easter Holidays as my excuse to get home. My family and friends were looking forward to me visiting for two weeks, and I was too. I hadn't seen anyone since our visit in January for Jac's birthday. Sabrina told me she'd made arrangements to visit her "pen-pal", Ben while I was away. I knew what was going to happen, but I didn't care. I just wanted to get home, and this was the perfect excuse. When my plane touched down at Prestwick Airport, I was so happy to see the grey clouds of Scotland and ecstatic to see my mum, my sister and Mary at the arrival gate to greet me. They made me feel welcome, loved and worthy of belonging just for being me!

I'd missed Christmas with my family that year, so my parents planned a Christmas in March. They'd brought the Christmas tree and the decorations out; Brian and his family were there; Christmas tunes and my friend, Melanie, who I hadn't seen in ages.

Melanie and I met when we were about fifteen when Brian was still finding himself and had a girlfriend called Nicola. I asked Brian if Nicola had any friends, and he and Nicola set up a double-date for us all. We arranged to go to the pictures to see The Invisible Man. I was smitten when Melanie arrived. Here was this beautiful girl with long, dark straight hair and perfect teeth and I was taking her out. Granted it was only at the cinema to watch a film, but that's what we did. I was timid at 15. I didn't make any of the "classic moves" I'd learned from films; I don't think I even attempted to hold her hand. The film was long, and I started work at 5 pm. I looked at my watch at 4:30 pm. I had to leave. I whispered into her ear that I had to go for work, and she turned her head towards me, and I kissed her. I then spent the rest of the night thinking about her. Nothing ever came of our relationship, but we did become good friends. She was that

relationship that should have happened, but the timing was never right: either I was single, and she had a boyfriend, or she was available, and I had a girlfriend. I was surprised that Melanie had come to the Christmas party considering we hadn't seen each other in about six years, but it was lovely to see her. We chatted, danced, sung and had a brilliant night!

Melanie (left) and me at our makeshift Christmas

Days later, my cousin, Christine, asked me if I wanted to go into town for a night out. I adore my cousin, and it was always a great night when we went out, so I was well up for it. I had started to think about Sabrina being on the other side of the country with another guy, so I needed something to take my mind off it. I asked Melanie if she wanted to come too because I really enjoyed her company, and thankfully she said yes. My sister came as well, as did some more of her and Christine's friends and we headed off to a karaoke bar. I love karaoke! It gives people the chance to perform and be someone else for 3 minutes at a time, but I also love it because I'm a good singer and I like to show that off. I tend to get a fair amount of attention when I sing as well, and I enjoy this. I feel accepted.

I remember Jackie and I have one of the best nights ever together. I hadn't seen my little sister in months, and I didn't realise how much I missed her. After the karaoke, we went to a nightclub. We danced until 2 am when Melanie came over to say she had to go home. I'd had a few drinks, so dared to ask her to stay out and stay with me. Being the sensible one, Melanie said no as she had Uni the next day. I knew that this could be mine and Melanie's last chance for something to happen. Forgetting about Sabrina and Ben for a split second, I took Melanie by the hand, moved towards her and kissed her for the second time in our lives. She then smiled at me and said, "Bye, Chris" and walked out of the club.

I had to go back to Germany. I could have stayed in Scotland, but when you're in an abusive relationship, you feel trapped. The distance and time apart had made me start to rethink things: maybe she'd changed? Perhaps nothing happened between her and Ben? No, I realised I was going to end up in the same situation if I didn't do something about it, so I decided to go back and tell her I needed to leave Germany. I couldn't say it was because I wanted out of the relationship; that would make her mad. I had to think of something else, so I lied. I told her that I'd got brilliant news and was offered a position at Strathclyde Uni as a lecturer in music. I had studied music at Strathclyde Uni, so it was slightly plausible (in my head anyway). It was a full-time position that paid well, so it just made sense to go back to Scotland – it was too good an opportunity to pass up. Sabrina agreed, and we decided we'd have a long-distance relationship.

When I got back, I didn't have a job. I was living with my parents and had no money, but that situation was better than living in Germany with Sabrina. I had worked in TGI's before leaving, so I was pretty sure I'd be able to get a job in hospitality. Frankie & Benny's had opened a new venue at The Fort in Glasgow, and I'd worked for them before, as a busser at the Quay. The assistant manager was now the manager of the new restaurant – score! He liked me, so I asked if he had a job available. I worked full-time and spent my time off on MSN Messenger talking to Sabrina – I wanted to make this long-distance relationship work, despite everything. (Distance makes the heart grow fonder.)

While at work, my mum used my computer and MSN used to sign you in automatically. A pop-up, "Hi Schatzi" appeared and my mum said, "Chris is at work Sabrina. I'll get him to message you when he's back." A conversation of some kind followed, and I got home to my mum asking why Sabrina thought I was a professor at a University. I couldn't tell my mum the shame I was feeling about the abusive relationship I was in, so I said Sabrina probably misunderstood. Eventually, I told Sabrina that the job at the university wasn't working out, so I'd changed careers and was now an assistant manager at Frankie and Benny's. This fable wasn't too far from the truth, although embellished - I was supervisor of the restaurant at this point, so far more believable than a music professor.

We were chatting on MSN one night, and I was trying to keep my eyes open, waiting for her to say I could go to sleep when she typed a message that filled me with dread.

"I want to come and visit you."

I wanted to say no! I wished to tell her that my life was perfectly happy with her at a distance. I didn't tell her what I thought, and within the week, she was heading to Scotland. My dad and I headed to Prestwick Airport to pick her up. Little did I know she'd only purchased a one-way ticket.

She told me after a week that she could only afford the one-way ticket so didn't have a plan to go home. I suggested that she come and work with me in Frankie's so she could save up for a ticket. She took this as me wanting to get rid of her, but I was only trying to help. Argument after argument (although "argument" would suggest more than one person talking), she decided to take the job offer, and she was working behind the bar at Frankie's where we could be together – all the time. It was Sabrina's first job, one of the most experienced bartenders trained her. Lisa helped Sabrina read the checks as they came through, and Sabrina spent most of the time pretending she couldn't understand them. I knew better. I learned how good her English was, and I knew she could read "Coke" and "Diet Coke". She didn't make any effort. It got to a point where she just refused to make the drinks, so the boss had no choice but to terminate her training. Her getting fired was my nightmare! She hadn't earned enough for her flight home, so while I was working, she'd be at my parents' house just waiting on me finishing.

After weeks of constant put-downs, belittling, arguments, and her saying she wanted to go home and didn't want to be with me, I booked her ticket home for the next day. I felt nervous about Sabrina going home; I wondered what it meant for our relationship. Did she not want to be with me anymore? Was I that desperate for love that I would continue with this unhealthy relationship? My mum took us to the airport, and she stayed in the car as I walked Sabrina to the gate. She turned to me and gave me a massive hug and said, "Ich Liebe Dich." (I love you). I said nothing. She went through the gate, walked out of Scotland, out of the UK and out of my life forever; she just didn't know it yet.

As soon as I got home, I ran to my room, opened my computer and my emails, and began to write a "break-up email" to Sabrina. It was polite, but stern. I can't remember it verbatim, but it brought light to how I'd felt over the last few weeks; how I didn't want to be with her anymore, and how the long-distance relationship wasn't working. I then blocked Sabrina on MSN, closed my emails and didn't open them for a fortnight. She didn't even bother to respond. I knew she received it (I knew her password and checked that she'd read it) and below my email was an email from Ben that told me everything I needed to know.

I was free! I had a new lease on life! I was in my early 20's, single and living it up! I felt great until those thoughts crept into the back of my mind, as per usual. Will I be single for the rest of my life? Will I ever be happy? Will I meet the love of my life? Little did I know, I already had.

5 FAMILY, AGAIN

The Duke family were your typical Catholic family; we were in abundance! My dad had six sisters and three brothers, and he was the youngest son. They all grew up and had their own families, and at one point, there were about sixty of us. My Granny and Granda Duke lived in a 5-apartment in Ruchazie in the East End of Glasgow. As a little boy, they lived in a mansion! Their house was MASSIVE!! It had three floors, four bedrooms, a huge living room that split into two, allowing space for a dining table. The kitchen was tiny; so tiny. This house became the hub for our family to meet, so we were there a lot. Celebrations, funerals, Friday nights – they all happened at my granny's. It was a treat when my Aunts, who'd moved to Livingston, came through for a Friday night at my Granny's too; that made it extra special.

A typical Friday look like this:

 – School in the morning

- From about p4 onwards, I was allowed to walk across the bridge over the M8 motorway (fun fact for you: it used to be a canal)

- Either my cousin Matthew, Christine, or my Granda Duke would meet me on the other side. It was usually my Granda, and I'd tell him all about school. He always listened, and when the conversation ended, he'd whistle the rest of the way.

- My mum would be there – if not down the Forge with my aunties. She'd be making dinner for whoever was coming that night. (My mum's macaroni was the best, I'm sure I mentioned this before.)

- While waiting on dinner, I'd be sitting watching all my favourite programmes on a Friday night: Play Days, Games Master, Fun House, Grange Hill, etc.

- Aunties and Uncles would arrive just in time for dinner, and in time for Neighbours. The grown-ups would sit at the table while the kids sat on the floor. We all watched Neighbours while we ate our dinner. After dinner (and Neighbours) there was always a fight about what to watch next. Everyone wanted to watch Home and Away, but my Granda wanted to watch the news; I don't think he ever won.

- After the soaps, the grown-ups would chat under a cloud of smoke and solve the world's problems together.

- I'd look out over the two gardens between my Granda's and my cousin Christine's to see if she was home. If so, I'd head over to hers because she was older, and she and her friends were cool. I thought I was too, just for talking to them.

- At 9 pm, Christine and her friends would be heading out, so I'd head back to my granny's where I'd find my Granda upstairs watching Friends, and the family would still be chatting until about half ten at night.

- They'd head home, and so would we.

I'd love to have a Friday night like that with them all again, just once.

We didn't see my mum's side of the family as much as we visited my dad's, but when we did, it was usually for longer. They lived on the East Coast of Scotland, which, to me, was hundreds and hundreds of miles away; really, it was half an hour on the M8 to Livingston. We'd stay for a few days or a week at a time; it was like a holiday. Boxing Day was one a favourite event at the Brough household. We called it Christmas Two because, after the excitement of Christmas Day in our own house, we'd head to Livingston on Boxing Day and have another Christmas. My mum's family are a lot smaller than the Duke side: four sisters and two brothers (still quite a large family, I'm told.) They'd be there, as would their children, so it was a family reunion every time. We'd have an exchange of gifts, another Christmas Dinner - I'm sure my mum made the trifle — and a party that went well into the "wee

My cousins, myself and my sister

hours". The cousins and I would get bored as the adults got drunker, so we'd sneak off to my Uncle Alan's room and watch TV, wrestle and just hang out; it was such a good time.

Unfortunately, there is a downside to having such a large family, and that is death and funerals. The first person I remember passing away was my big cousin Paul. I was very young at the time, and I remember finding out he died, but I don't remember much else. He was in his late teens. He was Christine's older brother. She was in primary school at the time, and she said she didn't process it as well as she could have – how do you process something like that the right way, though? Then my other big cousin, Matthew passed, Auntie Pat and then Uncle Billy. Matthew was Christine's other older brother, and Uncle Billy and Auntie Pat were her parents. Christine had lost every member of her immediate family before she was thirty years old. I looked up to her as a kid, and I felt proud to be "Christine's wee cousin". Christine has a beautiful family of her own now, including a grandbaby, and she continues to amaze me every day. Knowing she's gone through some of the awful tragedies a person can go

Christine (left) and I bonded from a very young age

through and suffer from a chronic illness and survive; I believe anything is possible.

The first time I remember the pain of someone in my family dying was my Granda Brough (my mum's dad). I was heading home from secondary school in November. It was cold and starting to get dark. As I walked up the street, needing to get home to heat up, I noticed a lot more cars in the street than usual. I just knew something was wrong. I had that gut feeling in the pit of my stomach. I, nervously, walked up the stairs to the flat and could smell the familiar smell of smoke as I got to the landing. I knew my family were inside. There was no outside handle to the door, so I always knocked to get in. My mum would greet me with a smile, but this time it was my Auntie Theresa who was looking very solemn. As I suspected, my family were there: my Granny Duke, my Auntie Ruby, Auntie Anna, I'm almost sure Christine was there too, and my Auntie Theresa who greeted me at the door. She took me to my bedroom, where Spice Girls posters covered the Coca Cola branded wallpaper, and said she had some bad news.

Two weeks before, we'd gone to visit my Granny and Granda in Livingston. We arrived, and the whole family were there again. As usual, the cousins snuck off to my Uncle Alan's room to hang out, and I'd noticed that people kept going into my Granda's room one at a

Visiting my Granny & Granda Brough in Livingston was always a treat

time. My mum came to me and asked me to go and say hi, so in I went and had a lovely chat with him. He was lying in his bed. I'd known he was poorly, but he just looked like my Granda. After our one-to-one, I gave him a hug and a kiss and went back to see my cousins; I didn't know that was the last time I'd speak to him.

My Auntie Theresa told me my Granda passed away; I just stood in silence. I didn't know what to do or say. She said to me that it was okay to cry and hugged me, but as much as that felt like the appropriate response, I just couldn't. I felt that lump in my throat but just couldn't let the tears out. Jackie was heartbroken; we all were. The funeral was a week later, and even then, I couldn't seem to cry. I sat at the back with my mum's friend while she and my dad were at the front. I remember seeing my mum walk past me at the end of the service and could see how devastated she was; my dad was holding her, supporting her. I went outside, and she reached out to me for a hug. The lump got more significant, but I still couldn't let go.

My Granda's funeral was the first one I'd attended, but it wouldn't be my last. Father Joe Sullivan had asked Mr McLean (music teacher) if he knew of anyone who'd be able to play the piano at mass on Sundays.

I was nominated and became St. Phillip's Church resident organist. Father Joe would let me play whenever I could, and not just practising hymns but also my schoolwork. The organ itself was this two-tiered, ancient electric organ where the seat was too low, and the organ was too high. I loved playing it. There was a lady who'd walk past me after taking her communion and say, "You're going to hurt yourself sitting like that. Sit up straight." I tried to no avail. A few months later, that lady passed away. I didn't even know her name, but I walked into the church one day to find a brand-new organ with a comfortable stool alongside it. Her family explained that she'd donated some money to the church to buy a new organ with a suitable seat to go with it; I was dumbfounded! This lady was a stranger, and she was so kind to her congregation and me. Her family explained that she'd been so concerned with my seating situation, and I was honoured to play at her funeral. I played with as much gusto as I could, on the new organ she'd donated, sitting on the comfy, suitable stool she'd made sure I had and made sure she had a service that celebrated her generosity. She was never far from my mind when I played in mass or other church services after that.

As I was the resident organist, I'd get one or two mornings off a week to play funerals in the parish. Mr McLean was okay with this, and one day, he asked me if I wanted to do an incredibly challenging funeral service: it was for a six-month-old baby. Mr McLean explained that although I'd become accustomed to distancing myself from the emotional side of funerals, children's funerals are different, and much,

much harder. He'd played for the victims in the Ice Cream Wars and some of the Lockerbie bombings, so he knew just how difficult it would be. Mr McLean explained what would happen throughout the service, what I would see and how he felt; that was the only funeral I declined to do.

When my Granny Duke passed away, I played at her funeral. She lived in Ruchazie, which meant the funeral would have been at St Phillip's, and there was no way I would let my Granny down by not playing and ensuring she had a great send-off. She always said she was very proud of my musical talent. I practised hard for her service and given a country song called "St Theresa of the Roses" to learn. I didn't know the tune to learn, and this was the days before any streaming service, so I went to HMV in Glasgow. They told me there was a store in England that had one copy of the album with this song on it. I ordered it and paid to get it sent to my house. Thankfully, it arrived two days before the funeral, and with the help of Iain Gordon, I learned it quickly.

I played at both my Granny & Granda Duke's funerals

I always wore my school uniform when I played (it was probably the smartest looking thing I owned), and it was no different at my Granny's funeral. I headed to the chapel earlier than the rest of my family to get another practice in - I had to be note-perfect. When it came time for her service, there were so many people there that most had to stand; she was such a loved and respected lady. Nevertheless, I had a job to do, and I had to concentrate on getting the music right. I'd got so used to distancing myself from the people at the funeral, and the emotional side of it, that I did the same at my Granny's. I saw my mum and my sister crying, but I just kept my head down and carried on doing my job.

I didn't sit with my family until the crematorium. I'd never been to a crematorium before, but I found it quite haunting, specifically when the red curtain closed on the coffin and that was that. I could hear the sobs of my Auntie Theresa down the front calling out for her mum. I sat there, not crying. As the end procession of "thanks for coming" hugs to the women and handshakes to the men went on, I saw the tears in my dad's eyes, his face contorted from the pain and heartbreak he felt from losing his mum that I realised big boys do cry! My dad is the strongest man I know, and to see him cry meant it was okay for me to do the same. Right away, the pressure I'd had on my shoulders lifted; that lump that had been residing in my throat at every sad moment for years, finally made its way out and I ran over to my dad and hugged him. I broke down. The tears flooded out, and I just held onto my dad; the relief I felt of letting the emotions out is a something I'll never forget.

I didn't play at many family funerals after my Granny's because I knew it was essential to sit with them and grieve properly. Unfortunately, death seemed to haunt our family for a while, with members seemingly passing away regularly. It got to a point where if my mum called out of the ordinary, I would answer with, "Who died this time?"

In a recent therapy session, we discussed the writing of this chapter and how I'd felt in doing so. My mood after bringing those memories to the forefront of my mind was low for a while. My therapist explained that I was mourning the loss of my granny, something I hadn't been able to do appropriately at her funeral as I was playing and focusing on the job, so I'm grateful that I've had the chance to reflect and grieve for her. I still have dreams that she comes back to life, and I spend the rest of the time worrying that she's going to leave again. I'm confident that if I have this dream now, I'll be a lot more comfortable with her leaving, and it'll feel more like she's just visiting.

6 A DIFFERENT KIND OF FAMILY

Newly single, after getting out of the abusive relationship, I was living with my parents, working as a restaurant supervisor and was happy; for the first time in what felt like a long time. I was also a reasonably flirty man, and this had its benefits. If a good-looking lady came in, I'd usually try to sit her in my section. Ladies left me their numbers on napkins, slipped them into my waistcoat pocket, asked friends to get mine, and while it was unquestionably an ego-boost, it wasn't what I wanted long-term. I'd started seeing one of the bartenders, Gemma. We got on like a house on fire: we laughed all the time; we made jokes; we were like best mates, but it fizzled out. I think we confused an intense friendship with something else.

My boss, Greg, ran the restaurant well: he'd make sure there was enough staff; sales were up because table turnover was quick; there was plenty of staff in the kitchen, and working was always fun and lucrative – ask anyone who is a waiter/waitress, they don't do it for the minimum wage! Greg's sister, Lisa, worked for the company too. She usually worked at The Quay but would occasionally be coerced into working at The Fort. I liked working with Lisa. The night Sabrina came back from Germany before she started working at Frankie's, I took her out to the restaurant for something to eat (splashing out with my 50% discount). Lisa served us, and I remember tipping her £10 to show off to Sabrina. Lisa worked at The Fort more and more, and I just waited for the day we were on shift together. Finally, that day arrived. We'd been flirting a little throughout the day, and I mentioned that my arms were itchy due to sunburn. Lisa scratched them as her nails were longer than mine, and a spark ignited; I was on her radar (she was already on mine).

Unfortunately, Lisa was moving to Dundee to study acting. It was about seventy miles away from where I was, and I was gutted. She worked weekends at The Fort although she lived in Dundee *(I mentioned the tips were that good, right?)* so she'd head back to Dundee on a Sunday evening. I remember on 25th September 2005, as I rode the number 38 bus from town to the East End, I decided to text Lisa to see how she was doing.

"Hey, how are you doing?"
"Hiya. I'm fine. Just in Glasgow waiting to get the bus back to Dundee. You?"
"How long have you got?"
"About an hour."
"You want some company?"

"Sure."

I didn't get off at my stop but paid for a ticket back into town and met Lisa at a bar under Queen Street Station. It was the first time we'd been in each other's company outside of work. I know it's not always the same in a different environment, but it didn't change how I felt. I was captivated by her. We had so much fun, and instead of getting her usual bus home, we decided that she'd get the early bus in the morning. The night became an impromptu date. We went to the Horseshoe bar where I knew they had karaoke *(a chance for me to show off my talent)*. I sang my favourite karaoke song at the time, Mustang Sally. It turns out Lisa has a thing for singers — might be something to do with the fact she isn't the best singer. I showed her the magic trick my Uncle Johnny had taught me: a trick where I could make ash appear on her hand without touching her *(she loves magic tricks)*, and we ended up in Campus — a student nightclub — and danced the night away; it was that night I realised I'd met the love of my life.

We spent the night together (my parents were away to Skegness that weekend) and I remember waking up to find her putting her shoes on. She said she was going to leave quietly to catch the bus, and she thought it was just a one-night thing. I wasn't going to give up that easily. I pulled her in for a hug and held her; I knew this was something special. The distance was an issue, but with her coming back to Glasgow at weekends to work, I made sure I was on shift with her, and we'd spend as much time together as possible. We began "seeing each other" just to see if we could make it work. I'd travel to Dundee to surprise her – this became something I'd do on my days off. I loved her company. She was such a kind person: she was funny, incredibly confident and beautiful, and I fell for her, hard. We decided it could

Lisa (left) and me

work, so we became "official" on 17th November 2005. I was so scared of losing Lisa that I did whatever I could to impress her. My self-sabotage habits began to rear their ugly heads. I had to make sure she knew how much I cared for her: I paid the bill every time we went out (she liked turn-about or 50/50); I'd buy her things just because they were expensive whether I thought she'd like them or now and I made up stories to impress her. I wasn't good enough for her just as I was, in my head, so I had to do whatever I could to make sure she'd not leave me. And so, I did what I did best: I lied.

One night I was out at Campus with my sister. They used to have the latest X Factor reject, Vengaboys, etc. in for gigs, and one night they had Peter Andre. Anyone of a certain age was very excited about this; it was Peter Andre! It was a ticketed event, and I was a fan of Andre in the '90s with "Mysterious Girl" being my number one song. I didn't want to miss it, so I'd gone to a karaoke competition the week before where the top prize was tickets to Campus to see him. Just the ticket, I thought! I won after including the rap part in the song and got to see him live.

I still don't know why, but I embellished this story, massively to Lisa. I had to impress her. I told her that someone had informed Peter Andre of my rendition of "Mysterious Girl", and he was so impressed that he invited me up on stage at Campus to sing with him. I'd fabricated this bullshit story, and she believed me. It wasn't until she spoke to my sister and said, "It must have been pretty cool to see your big brother singing with Peter Andre" and Jackie just shaking her head and scoffing that she realised it was rubbish. I took her by the hand, led her into my room, and she just looked at me confused, and mad. She asked me why I'd lied about something as outrageous as that, but I couldn't answer. "To impress you" didn't seem like a good enough reason to cause her any pain, and it wasn't until years later that I managed to explain that my anxieties and self-doubt caused me to lie. The disappointment and hurt in her eyes are something I'll always remember. She forgave me, after giving me a chance to come clean with any other lies I'd told, and I realised how remarkable she is and found myself falling madly in love with her.

Eventually, we moved in together to her flat in Dundee. I struggled to get a job as I couldn't work full-time in Glasgow and live in Dundee as I didn't drive. In almost 5 years, we'd gone through about 25 years' worth of relationship trouble, mainly due to financial issues. We'd struggled to pay rent, council tax, struggled to afford our weekly food shop and been evicted from a property. It was a tough time for both of us, and with Lisa studying full-time, she was working part-time (some weeks full-time in Pizza Hut on the Kingsway in Dundee), and we weren't making ends meet. I managed to start working as a DJ for an agency, but working nights wasn't ideal. My mental health issues were causing me all sorts of problems in trying to get work during the day, but no matter how little we had, I always found enough to pay for cigarettes *(about £7 a day then)*. This cost was more than our weekly shop for both of us.

Lisa went to university in Sunderland after finishing her studying in Dundee, and, naturally, I went with her. I couldn't find a job there either, but she was working on weekends at Frankie's at The Gate in Newcastle. I'd burnt my bridges with the company, so couldn't be employed by them. Lisa was studying BA Hons in Drama and English, working full-time, directing and performing in shows, and I wasn't doing anything to contribute. There was a lot of friction and resentment brewing in our relationship, and Lisa ended our relationship many times but was always "won over" by promises of change. I didn't want to lose her. She was the absolute love of my life; the person I'd been looking for, and she loved me for being me. It was a week before Lisa finished Uni, and I'd been in touch with someone who was looking for a DJ in Corfu, so I suggested we take a break and head for sunnier climates before we "grew up" and became boring adults. Lisa agreed, and I headed out, and she followed two weeks later when her studies ended. At first, we had a great time: the staff were lovely at the hotel we were in; the tourists were great fun; we were treated well by the owner, and we were enjoying each other's company again. I was working as the hotel entertainer, and Lisa worked in a waffle shack on the beachfront. She worked from 4 pm until midnight, and I worked days at poolside and nights in the bar. It was good fun. Unfortunately, it didn't last.

As the season got busier, the hotel owner moved us from an empty apartment to something best described as a hovel under the rooms. It was so bad it spewed shit at us if enough people went to the loo that day, and there was no way of clearing it. We just had to wait until the drainage system worked its way through it. The staff started treating us differently and the receptionist, in particular, became quite nasty. It became a place where everyone gossiped about everyone else, and the fantasy of working abroad had worn off. *There is one particular memory of this place that is a good one, but I'll talk about it later.* I injured myself by the pool, and the hotel Doctor yanked my foot so hard I ended up on crutches; he thought my ankle was dislocated *(it wasn't)*. The first thing the owner asked was, "You're still working tonight, right?" although I could barely stand. Lisa didn't know what had happened until she arrived at the bar after her shift around 12:30 am. She saw me standing on crutches and asked for a stool so I could sit down and keep the weight off my ankle. I wasn't allowed because the owner said it made me look sloppy. That night, Lisa asked a crucial question. She said, "Are we happy here?" We knew the answer, and we knew we could control that happiness, so we decided to arrange to go home.

When we moved to Abronhill, Cumbernauld, we'd been together for five years. We'd had a pregnancy scare that turned out to be negative. We both felt disappointed, so decided that Lisa would come off her birth control. Three months later, Lisa was pregnant. To say we were shocked would be an understatement, as we didn't expect to happen that quickly, but we felt excited. Lisa came running downstairs at 2 am with a positive pregnancy test telling me we were going to be parents. I couldn't believe it. I'd always wanted to be a dad, even when I was a wee boy.

We moved into Lisa's Gran and Papa's house, in Kilsyth, as the flat we were in wasn't exactly "child-friendly". We loved Kilsyth. We loved the friends we made, and the area, in general, was so welcoming. Lisa's heartburn was so severe the doctors prescribed her with two massive bottles of Gaviscon: one sat on her bedside table, and the other was with her at all times. About four months before our baby was due, I suggested we got married. I said, "It would be nice if we all had the same last name" and her reply was, "Is that your way of proposing?"

This wasn't the first time I'd proposed.

Proposal 1)

A collage of photographs featuring the two of us played to the song "Forever" by The Beach Boys on Bebo.

Proposal 2)

We went to WWE in London and were featured on the segment The Kiss Cam hosted by Maria (a WWE diva). I spotted a camera operator point their camera towards us, so

Front row at WWE

as soon as I saw our faces on the big screen, I got down on one knee and proposed. "Oh my god! He just asked her to marry him!" Maria said. She didn't respond to this one. She hugged me and kissed me, and that was good enough for me.

Proposal 3) *(that memory from Greece I mentioned).*

The hotel we were staying in had a gorgeous cliff-top restaurant, and I'd asked the Maître d to hold the best table for us that night. It was one of the loveliest spots of Sidari, and I'd decided I would propose just as the sun was setting. I could see it slowly go behind the horizon, but I just couldn't work up the nerve to do it – this one felt more real than the others! Just as we were about to go into nightfall, I plucked up the courage, got down on one knee and presented her with an understated, white gold ring with small diamonds going across the front of the band – perfect for her. This time, she said yes. Lisa's not one for being outwardly expressive (not before kids anyway), and she smiled, but the lady at the table beside us was in bits, as she passed on her congratulations through tears; that proposal was perfect.

We decided to go ahead and get married before our baby was born, and we had about six weeks to plan it. We booked a Wednesday because that was 17th November, which meant we were getting married the day we became an official couple. It also gave us three weeks on the other side of the wedding to finalise getting things for the baby's arrival. Lisa had been off work due to pregnancy complications (baby was fine but her hips had rotated so she couldn't waitress) so she was to rest. I took on the responsibility to plan our intimate ceremony at Park Circus in Glasgow. At 2 pm, on

Wednesday, 17th November 2010, we became husband and wife in front of twenty of our closest family and friends. We then went to our favourite restaurant in Kilsyth for the meal, and we shared stories, did the speeches and had an incredible time. Throughout the meal, Lisa kept getting off her chair to walk about. She couldn't sit still, as she felt so uncomfortable. She even changed into a pair of trainers as her feet were in agony.

Lisa's best friends and her sister had gifted us a night at the Castlecary

Hotel where they'd spread rose petals over the bed, had Irn Bru instead of champagne (still had the champagne glasses) and surprised us with this at the end of the evening. There was a bath with jacuzzi features in the bathroom, and that was the first place Lisa wanted to go. Sharing was out of the question as she was so pregnant and I was overweight, so she went first. I sat on the edge as we chatted about the day, pressed the jets and got swiftly told off because that's not a good idea when you're pregnant. Due to her being so uncomfortable, she didn't eat much of the meal, so we ordered a pizza. Lisa got out, got her PJs on and I ran my bath – I was knackered too (obviously not as much). I got into a steaming hot bath, pressed the jets and lay back to enjoy the feeling of the pressure hit my back. Lisa came in to chat to me, and as she stepped into the bathroom, she sneezed. She looked down to find her trousers soaked! She said, "my waters just broke". Well, I sprang into action! I leapt out the bath, grabbed a towel, wrapped it around my waist in one smooth motion, called her dad to pick up the hospital bag while sitting with her telling her everything was going to be okay. **Did I bollocks!!** I phoned my mum!!!! I told her Lisa's waters had broken and my mum said, "Okay, is she okay? Have you phoned the hospital?" I said, "No! I phoned you!" My mum laughed at me, told me to hang up and call the hospital and call Lisa's dad to pick up the hospital bag.

While I was doing this, Lisa had got changed, cancelled the pizza and started to get everything organised to head out of the hotel. In what felt like a minute, we were driving along the motorway in Lisa's Dad's car with her mum, her dad, Lisa and me heading to the hospital. At 6:41 am, Alyssa was born, and we tell her how she gate-crashed our wedding. She was the best wedding present ever!

Mummy, Daddy and our little wedding crasher

Lisa and I have been through a lot in the past fifteen years. My Depression and my mistakes have tried to ruin our relationship, many times. We handled a lot of my problems poorly, due to our ignorance regarding mental health issues. We continue to learn more about this every day. Had I not met Lisa, I have no idea where I'd be, or if I'd made it through those darkest of times.

Fifteen years, three children, two dogs, three business partnerships and everything in between and we're still together; still going strong.

7 PARENTHOOD

When I was a little boy, there were four things I wanted to be when I grew up: a dad, a radio host, a wrestler and an author. When Alyssa was born, I should have been over the moon; after all, that was one of my life goals achieved, but I wasn't. I felt so guilty because I didn't get the rush of love I'd been told about when you hold your baby for the first time. All the fathers in my life were providers, and I thought they were excellent dads. My dad worked seven days a week; my Granda's worked and provided for their large families; Lisa's dad, Gordon, was working four jobs at one point to ensure he could provide for his children, so I felt so much pressure to live up to the standard they'd set. At the time Alyssa was born, I was working in an electrical shop as a salesperson. I had no passion for the job, and my boss had no compassion for his employees' mental health. When I'd been diagnosed with Depression, I handed him my sick line, and he said, "I've already got people off with a real illness. I don't need this as well." Mentally, I was fragile. Comments like that only added to my feelings of inadequacy and failure. (*These experiences are a reason I advocate mental health awareness now; they're dangerous!)*

If you're a parent, you'll know of this questionnaire the Health Visitor does about a week after the baby arrives. They run through a set of questions to help determine whether the mother is needing some extra help and support and to help detect post-natal Depression. Whatever Lisa answered, I answered the opposite:

1. I have been able to laugh and see the funny side of things?
Lisa: "Yes"
Me: "No"

2. I have looked forward with enjoyment to things?
Lisa: "Yes"
Me: "No"

3. I have blamed myself unnecessarily when things went wrong?
Lisa: "No"
Me: "Yes"

4. I have been anxious or worried for no good reason?
Lisa: "No"
Me: "Yes"

5. I have felt scared or panicky for no very good reason?

Lisa: "No"

Me: "Yes"

6. Things have been getting on top of me?

Lisa: "No"

Me: "Yes"

7. I have been so unhappy that I have had difficulty sleeping?

Lisa: "No"

Me: "Yes"

8. I have felt sad or miserable?

Lisa: "No"

Me: "Yes"

9. I have been so unhappy that I have been crying?

Lisa: "No"

Me: "No" (I wouldn't outwardly cry)

10. The thought of harming myself has occurred to me?

Lisa: "No"

Me: "Yes"

Although I was working full-time in a job I despised, I still couldn't afford our house, grocery shopping, baby supplies and, as far as I was concerned, that made me a terrible father. To combat this feeling of inadequacy, I'd buy "stuff". I liked owning "stuff". I thought if I had the best TV, the latest iPhone, the top of the range Blu Ray player, a new sofa and so on, then I was providing. I was able to get the best of the best, which meant I was a good father. The issue is, I couldn't afford the "stuff", so it went on credit. I'd made poor financial choices from eighteen years old when I received "free money". I'd maxed out credit cards, store cards, etc., and my credit rating was abysmal. My score meant the only line of credit I was eligible for was from Pay-Day loan companies and pay weekly stores. Lisa would ask where it came from, and I'd spin some bull-crap excuse and would repay the over-inflated prices weekly, leaving us in deficit. Then I'd get more out on loan, and the vicious cycle would start again.

I also have a food issue. Have you ever seen the TV show Secret Eaters? Well, that was me. I'd get up in the morning, have tea and toast, then head to the bus for work. I'd pop into the newsagents and get some crisps and a bottle of Coke. If the bakery were open, I'd also grab a bacon roll. At lunch, I'd head to the supermarket on the industrial site and buy a box of cheesy pasta (serves 3). I'd have the whole packet for my lunch. After work, I'd head home, and the driver would let me off just outside the chip shop. I'd get a single king rib, a steak pie and walk the rest of the way home where Lisa would have prepared dinner for me. Honestly, was it any wonder why I couldn't provide for my family when all the money was being eaten or going on unnecessary rubbish?

Lisa had had enough of my lies. She knew something was going on as a weekly pay store kept phoning to discuss my account. They wouldn't divulge any information other than saying I had to get in touch, but they always called when I was at work. I never called them when I was at home, and always avoided Lisa's reminders too. I couldn't afford to pay them back, so avoiding them seemed to be the best solution at that time. Lisa and I would argue about it all the time, but I am so good at lying. I'd always convince her that there must be some kind of mistake. We'd had Summer by this point, so she had two children to look after; mainly on her own because I had to work as a DJ at nights in an attempt to earn more money, and she worked weekends. We didn't see each other a lot, which is probably the only reason it went on for so long.

I'd let it go on too long, and the company came to the door to remove the furniture. Everything imploded. Lisa was humiliated. She was embarrassed that she had believed me; angry that I'd lied to her and ashamed to have these strangers at the door with a white van to remove furniture she thought was purchased in full. Lisa went to the only person who knew me as well as she, my mum. She told my parents what was going on and said she didn't know what to do. My mum said, "If Jacqueline came to me saying the same thing, I'd tell her to leave. Just because it's my son doesn't mean I should give different advice: leave him." My mum saw how miserable Lisa had become and was encouraging her to leave me. Lisa told me she was at my parents' house, so I drove over to talk to her. She was so sad; heartbroken that I'd lied to her again, and for so long when she'd given me so many chances to come clean; so many opportunities to let her help me out of the situation I'd got myself into, and I didn't take any of them. Lisa went into the other room to change one of the girls' nappies and left my dad and me alone. My dad looked at me and said, "If I lose those girls because of you, I will never forgive you." That was it. That was the words that shook me to my core. I was on the verge of losing everything: my wife, my children, my parents, everything that meant the most to me in the world. I realised all the "stuff" I'd purchased meant nothing; they didn't define me or make me a good father and husband; being a partner and honesty made me what I wanted to be. Lisa and I spoke, a lot, and she said the only way she'd consider staying with me is if I went to the doctor and got help for everything. I did, and I'm so glad.

I sat in the waiting room, feeling very nervous, as I watched the second-hand move around the clock face. "Christopher Duke. Room ten", said the internal sound system. I took a deep breath in and headed towards Doctor McGregor's room. I knocked.

"Come in," said the doctor.

I spoke to Dr McGregor and was diagnosed with post-natal Depression; something I didn't think men could get. It was a mixture of setting my standard too high and the pressure of becoming a husband and a father in twenty-four hours that set it all off. I had a lot of work to do, and it started with being very honest with Lisa – it was time to change things.

Since doing this, I've been able to tell Lisa a lot about what was going through my head at that time in my life, and she's been very patient and sympathetic – one of the reasons she's bloody awesome! She has said that if I'd told her of the financial situation, she'd have helped – likely after "going nuts at me" but we'd have got through it together. I wish I'd taken that argument instead of waiting until I had no choice and almost lost everything.

8 CAREER

Radio had always been a passion of mine since I was as young as I can remember. I found it fascinating that someone could be sitting in front of a microphone chatting to millions listeners, but still make me feel like I was on the only one. When I was ten, I'd sit under my duvet with a torch listening to Tiger Tim early evening and switch to Radio Two, Scotland, where Scotty McClue would take me through to midnight, on a hand-held, battery-powered radio.

Career Day was when we'd get visitors coming to our school to tell us what they do for a living. I remember the local police, the lady who worked at the counter at the shop and the person who put the lights in on the top floor of the high-rise flats; we could see them out the classroom window. In primary 6, George Bowie came to our school. He was on Radio Clyde and a big deal!! A famous person had never come to St. Modan's Primary before! I sat, cross-legged, on the hard gym floor taking in every word he said. It felt like he was talking to me only.

George Bowie finished his talk, and as he made his way out, all the girls from the upper classes ran towards him with a piece of paper for him to autograph. I decided that day I wanted to be a radio presenter. I went home and pulled out two cassette players from my dad's cupboard. I found a blank one from my mum's suitcase of cassette tapes, put it in one of the players, inserted a tape in the other player and hit record. "This is Chris Duke from Duke FM ready to play you some of the biggest hits from the glam rock ages. Starting us off: it's not lion feet...it's not elephant feet... it's TIGER FEET!" I pressed play on the other cassette player and turned it so the first cassette player could pick it up as Tiger Feet by Mud played. I subjected my parents to every single show, and when we were on a long car journey, I'd bring my tape along and ask them to turn Clyde Two off so they could hear the latest show from Duke FM.

I also wrote to our local radio station, frequently, asking for work. I had no idea what a demo tape was, but I wrote in with ideas of what I would do if I were on the radio – clearly no consideration for how arrogant I must have sounded. Anyway, when I was fifteen, I wrote to the programme controller at Radio Clyde and suggested the local children of Glasgow have a "Homework Hour". It would be an hour where I would host, obviously, and the children of the city could call in with homework, upcoming exam questions. I'd have a special guest: teachers from different schools with specific areas of expertise. I received a reply.

"Dear Christopher,

This has to be one of the most unique "Can I get a job?" letters I've ever received..." and that was the most positive part of their response. The rest was pretty much a "that's not how you get into the radio" type of reply.

Thankfully, the knowledge of how to get into radio became more known to me as I got older. I found a local radio station where I volunteered and got on air as often as I could. I had a weekend show at Pulse FM in Paisley, and I'd do everything I could think of to make my show as unique as possible. I thought my shows were worthy, so I'd take samples and turn it into a demo and send it to every radio station in the country. I'd also phone the stations and ask if they'd listened to my tape; most hadn't, and if they had, they weren't "looking".

When Lisa and I moved to Dundee, one of the jobs I'd got was working in Cash Converters. It was in this job that I discovered Dundee's local radio station: Wave 102. I'd spend months listening to the voices of Dundee radio, and when we both started working in a local karaoke club called Starz, the host was Dave Moran, who just happened to be the breakfast presenter on, you guessed it, Wave 102. He was also the programme controller for the station, and I'd plucked up the courage to have a chat with him. He was very kind, and I remember thinking his voice was far more familiar than his face, and how cool that was. His advice was the same as everyone else in radio, "when you're ready, send me a demo, and we can chat."

It was a few years later, Lisa and I were living in Cumbernauld before I felt my demo was "ready", and I attached it to an email and sent it to Dave. I felt very nervous waiting on his response, but this was the closest I'd even been to stepping foot in a radio station. I didn't have a phone back then, so I'd check my email daily. I logged into my Hotmail account with my super-secret password "pa55word" and waited on my inbox to load. There, at the top of the list was an email marked "sender: Wave 102". AAAARRRRGGGGHHH!! They'd replied!!! I clicked the email:

The response from the remote server was:
550 5.1.1 dave@wave102.co.uk Recipient not found.

Damn it! My way into Dundee's Wave 102 was gone, I thought. Moran had left the station a year before I sent my demo, and he'd never got to hear it. I kept going. I contacted the new programme controller, Alistair Smith. I emailed him explaining why I loved Dundee so much, why I wanted to be on the radio, and why I wanted to work at Wave 102. I emailed and called him at least once a week for a year before getting a response,

"Chris.

Why don't you come up and see me next week and we can have a chat in person?"

Oh. My. Goodness! My mind started going a mile a minute, again, asking why he wanted to see me in person. Was he going to offer me a show? Was I good enough? I couldn't sleep for the week leading up to the meeting, and when it arrived, it was very relaxed (which helped). We sat and had a cup of tea discussing our love for radio and why we were so passionate about Dundee. He couldn't offer me anything permanent due to having an already full schedule, but he was planning on going on holiday for a fortnight in a month. He was looking for someone to cover him and offered to train me ahead of this so I'd be ready to go on for him should I be good enough. I'd also be paid, which was a big difference to community radio. During our training, I listened to everything Alistair had to teach. I was like a sponge. I absorbed as much information as I could for that week.

My first show came and went so quickly; I can barely remember it. I do remember everyone in the office being so lovely, wishing me luck, and saying to call if I needed any help.

I also remember discussing two stories: one was as I was heading to the station that morning, holding a macaroni pie, ready to eat as I hadn't had breakfast yet. As I was looking forward to the first bite of calorific delight, I felt a thud on the back of my head, and before I could appreciate what had happened, my cheese-filled crusty beauty was soaring into the sky in the beak of a seagull! The second story was the moment I had in the studio. I was playing one of my favourite songs "The One and Only" by Chesney Hawkes, and I'd just sat back in the worn-out chair and took it all in the sound of the song, the glow of the "on-air" light shining in my eyes, and I smiled. I realised I had gone from a wee boy playing with cassette tapes broadcasting to my living room to a grown-up having the opportunity to work in a well-established radio station that broadcast to an entire city.

The two weeks flew by, and before I knew it, Alistair was back from his holiday. I'd had a taste for it now, though. I knew I wanted to do it again. I became the go-to cover guy for Wave 102 for about a year until Gary, the breakfast host, announced he was leaving. There was finally a radio slot available! The breakfast show is THE SHOW most presenters want. I put together a PowerPoint presentation for Alistair explaining why I was the perfect person for the job. We scheduled a meeting, and I was determined not to leave without that position.

We were living in Cumbernauld, which is about 70 miles from Dundee, so I was commuting during the cover shifts. The fuel cost was a small fortune (a daily 140 miles round-trip is not fun when finances are tight). At this point in our personal lives, we had Alyssa and Summer, so Lisa was pretty much a single parent while I was chasing this dream. We decided it would be more cost-effective and more efficient for Lisa to get the kids around if I had my own car. I got a left-hand drive, bright yellow, two-seater Smart car. It cost £20 for a week's worth of travel from Cumbernauld to the City of Discovery compared to about £120.

The day of my presentation, I'd put on my best suit, trimmed my beard, and hopped into my glorified Go-Kart and headed up the A9. As I was passing the Wallace Monument at Stirling, I heard a BANG and my car tilted to one side. I moved over the hard shoulder as it rumbled across the lane. I'd had a blow-out. Why today? Of all days, why today? I called breakdown recovery and explained, but because it was a smart car, finding a suitable tyre was a challenge, so I had no choice but to miss the meeting. Thankfully, Alistair understood and was kind, but in my head, I knew this had cost me my first full-time position at Wave 102.

A few days later, Alistair called and explained I didn't get the breakfast position, but not because of the blow-out. He didn't think I was ready for that show and had a lot more learning to do. I was disappointed. He went on to say he was going to take the breakfast show but needed someone to do drive time, and he offered me that role instead. My disappointment turned to delight. I had an absolute blast working on drive time: the banter with the travel reporters was always fun; keeping people company on their way home from work, and the listeners engaging with me was the best part.

Radio is a cut-throat industry: there's always someone just behind you gunning for your job, and if you don't perform well and bring in the listeners, you lose your job. Paul replaced Alistair; he had a wealth of knowledge and experience from working on the more well-known stations in Scotland and was the new programme controller. I felt sad for Alistair. He'd worked so hard to build up Wave 102 in Dundee, and I just found it harsh that he lost it so quickly in such a brutal manner. However, "that's showbiz." As new programme controller, it's known that they come in and shake things up, generally by firing someone. I was last in so figured I'd be first out. I have no shame in admitting I sucked up to the new boss. I found his name on Twitter and connected with him.

We started chatting, and I made my intentions clear that I wanted the breakfast show. Whatever Paul's plan was, he kept it to himself. The only thing we knew was a date where changes would take effect, and as that date got closer, the rest of us got nervous. The date arrived, Paul and Adam (the station's owner) took us into the boardroom one-by-one. Dave Price, a local legend who'd been with Wave 102 since it launched, went first. Ten minutes later, he came out, sat at his desk and said, "That's it all over for me." We were shocked. This was Dave Price – we thought he was untouchable! I was next. I thought there is no way I'd be staying if they let Dave Price go, so I went in fully expecting what I would have considered the worst possible news. They did what I expected and took me off drive-time. I thought "It was fun while it lasted". They continued to say they were removing me from drive time to host the new "Chris Duke at Breakfast Radio Show". WHAT THE?! I was utterly astonished; my dreams had come true - I couldn't believe it! Everything I'd worked to achieve over the last few years was coming to fruition. Paul moved Alistair to mid-morning, and Paul was on drive-time.

The next couple of years were a bit of a whirlwind, but there are specific opportunities I was afforded that stand out. Three stories in particular.

Jamie Dornan

The press was invited to Alfred Dunhill Links Tournament every year, which was a pro-am golf tournament where some of the most famous celebs would come to Saint Andrew's to play with the professionals. The year I went had Hugh Grant, Ronan Keating, Greg Kinnear, but the one celeb I HAD to meet was Jamie Dornan (50 Shades of Grey star). The other stations had managed to get an interview with the different stars, but no one had managed to get Dornan – challenge accepted! I waited by the 18th hole, and as he approached the press area, a sea of microphones appeared and pushed me out the way as he interviewed for the tournament website. They were talking "birdies" and "pars" and other words I didn't care to understand, and I waited for his interview to end. As soon as it did, he was accosted by other press who were throwing questions at him from every angle, and I just stood at the back and waited a little more. The crowd cleared as he headed to the private playing area, and I said, "Jamie, a quick word for Wave 102?"

"As long as it's quick," he said as he was keen to rest. I know nothing about golf, so I wondered what I could ask him. "I...eh, Jamie..." I stumbled, "I notice you're sporting a very nice, thick and manly beard there. Being one of the most handsome men in the world, I have a question for you..." I got my phone out of my pocket and

One of the sexiest men on the planet...and Jamie Dornan

showed him a picture of myself with a beard. "Last week I shaved my beard off for the first time in years – my wife prefers the beard – what are your thoughts: beard or no beard?"

"Oh, my word!" he said in his thick Irish accent, "Beard. Always beard. You're much more handsome with your beard." He grabbed my face, which was a little blushed at this point, and continued, "Look at this baby-faced boy. You're all man when you have a beard." "There you have it," I said, "Jamie says beard: the beard is coming back." I wrapped up the 30-second interview, thanked him and off he went.

Mel C

As I was preparing for the next day's show, Paul came up to me and said, "Chris, do you have plans tonight?" Lisa was pregnant with our third child, so I had no plans other than to go home to her and the kids. "Oh well, I suppose I need to interview Mel C myself?" he said, jokingly. He had my attention! I was a HUGE Spice Girl fan (a Spice Boy) growing up, and there was no way I could miss the chance to interview one of my idols.

After a quick phone call, I managed to organise a babysitter for the kids and Lisa, and I went to interview Mel C together. Paul gave me instructions, and I spent the rest of the day thinking how I could "spice" up the interview to make it memorable; not only for our listeners and me but also for Mel. I wasn't supposed to alter anything. There's a formula most radio companies use to increase their listenership, which is excellent, but it stunts the more think-outside-the-box presenters who I idolised. Chris Moyles is one of them, but I didn't want to be another Chris Moyles; I wanted to be the first Chris Duke. Wave 102 was following this formula to grow their station and having Mel C would most definitely bring in new listeners, but my ego wanted something more. Lisa and I arrived, and I was so excited and ready to go, reminding her to record the interview – for the millionth time. There was a lady from BBC Scotland and me interviewing Mel C, and she went first. It was the typical "Desert Island Discs" interview: what's your favourite album? Who inspired you growing up? I started to doubt what I had planned; I hadn't thought about any of those types of questions.

The time had come. Lisa and I were ushered over to a separate bar area to sit next to Melanie Chisholm, the Sport Spice Superstar herself, and start the interview. I introduced myself and Lisa, and she was unbelievably friendly. We bonded over parenthood, as Mel spoke about her daughter, Scarlett, and I told of my girls. Lisa commented on her Wonder Woman T-Shirt, which she loved, and she was just so pleasant; she put me at ease right away. The interview went well. We discussed her Spice Girl days; the possibility of there being a reunion tour, and when she spotted the strap on my shoulder, said, "Is that a ukulele?" I'd chickened out of my plan, but she'd seen it. I had no choice now and thought "just do it". I pulled it out the bag and said, "yeah, it's my friend's." She commented on how lovely it was and asked

That time I sang with a Spice Girl

if I could play it. "Well, Melanie. I can play three chords on this ukulele, and those three chords just happen to be the same three chords in "When You're Gone" with you and Bryan Adams. I was going to suggest that we did something a bit different, so how about I be Bryan Adams, you be you, and we have a wee sing-song?"

She smiled. She said, "Go for it!" We sang a verse and a chorus of that song, and it wasn't a polished performance, obviously, but it was brilliant in spite of that, and I love that I can say I have sung with a Spice Girl.

Olly Murs

A month before the end of my time at Wave 102, Olly Murs was coming to Dundee to perform at Slessor Gardens. Instead of the rival station, the event organisers asked Wave 102 to host the event! The whole team were over the moon. Being the hosting station, we got a pre-recorded interview with Olly Murs lasting fifteen minutes and were the opening act for the crowd at the concert. I was awarded both opportunities and turned fifteen minutes into a one-hour guest slot with him - done through creative links (radio term for the speaking between songs) and, I entertained the audience the best way I know. It wasn't until I finished that the manager of the event informed me, I was there to play background music only – oops! Jordan, our producer, and I went backstage, and we could hear the roars of the audience waiting on Olly getting louder and louder; we could feel the electricity buzzing through us as the excitement built up. Jordan handed me a mic, and I could feel the energy pumping through my body. I turned to Jordan and said, "Follow my lead." I walked onto the stage, in front of 10,000 people, who roared with approval at seeing something happening. I introduced myself and Jordan and said we were going to be entertaining the crowd before Louisa Johnson (the current X Factor runner-up) came on to perform. "Uptown Funk" by Bruno Mars played over the speakers, and 10,000 people started jumping up and down, dancing and having a great time. I spotted my mum and Mary beaming up at me with pride.

Paul had said he wanted me to play up-to-date tunes and do some mixing – I wasn't very good at mixing, or following instructions, as the next thing I did was get as many people as I could in the biggest YMCA dance that had ever hit the North East of Scotland. Then it was Bon Jovi's Living on a Prayer where I sang "Oh we're halfway there", and

the audience sang, "Oh! Oh! Living on a Prayer" and ending with me shouting "What's your favourite radio station in

Performing in front of 10,000 people proves that you can achieve anything

Dundee?" to 10,000 replies of, "WAVE 102!" I was having the time of my life! Louisa Johnson came on, and that was my time up, but the aftermath was incredible. I had people asking me for selfies and autographs, banter with members of the crowd. I felt like a superstar. A little boy came up to me while I was getting some chips and said I inspired him, that was the cherry on the icing on the cake. He made it all worthwhile!

These stories helped me realised that I could make things happen. I had been given these incredible opportunities, but I could still make them into something more. When I interviewed Jamie Dornan, my negative thoughts started: I don't know anything about golf; I'm going to look like an idiot; he's not going to be interested in what I have to say. However, I found something to talk about and went with it, and it was one of my favourite thirty-second interviews. When I went to interview Mel C, the self-doubt crept in, again: this interview wouldn't be special; she won't sing with you; you'll embarrass yourself, but I decided to ignore those thoughts and go for it. After all, what was the worst that could happen? When I stood at the side of the stage at the Olly Murs concert, my thoughts went to no one is here to see you; don't bother with the entertainment side, just play music and go home. I didn't listen to it that time either, thankfully.

Unfortunately, my time at Wave 102 came to an abrupt end. Paul asked me to pre-record the last hour of my show one day and go into the boardroom. The night before, Adam, the station owner, had sent an email saying he wanted to meet with everyone the following day, so there was an element of concern in the air. The apprehension was validated when they said that would be my last hour on Wave 102. I left the station feeling bitter, angry and resentful. They asked me to move my family up, so how could they do this to me when I'd worked my butt off to increase their listenership so much? I was angry, and felt like I'd let my family down, especially Lisa. I'd convinced her to move away from her friends and family to support me and I'd lost it all. Thankfully, my attitude to this experience has changed with time. When I look back at the radio now, I look back at my time fondly. I remember those moments where I made something extraordinary happen, the friends I made and the impact I had on that little boy who was inspired to be more confident in himself – all of those things made that part of my radio career worth it. Now, the decision I had to wrestle with was what to do next.

9 CLANG!

There is an ongoing joke between my friends and me, that whenever I happen to mention a famous person's name that I've interacted with, they reply in unison with, "Clang"! The joke being that I just "dropped" a celebrity's name. Throughout my life, I have been fortunate to meet some famous people I admire and interact with them in ways not many people have. I just wanted to share with you a couple of stories that may include someone you know very well: CLANG!

John Stamos

John Stamos is probably best known worldwide for his role as Uncle Jessie in Full House or Fuller House, and while you might not remember him from this, he also played Zack in Friends. Remember when Monica and Chandler were looking for a sperm donor, and Chandler invited his friend from work? That guy. He also sings regularly with The Beach Boys, and this is how we met him.

The Beach Boys were coming to Montrose Music Festival in 2017, and John Stamos was coming with them. Lisa and I loved Full House, and I took the opportunity to interview John on the radio to help promote the concert.

He was lovely. John called me early in the evening, and we had a great chat about his career so far. I also told him about the time I proposed to Lisa using his song "Forever", and it was at that point Stamos asked if he could speak to her. Lisa's face went bright red, and he suggested we call our soon-to-be-born baby Jessie, after his Full House character.

We were given complimentary tickets to The Beach Boys gig, so we took the chance to get out before we became parents to three children. It was a great night. Lisa and I kept talking about how laid back it was and how everyone attending was just having a great time. John Stamos played a few songs on guitar and drums as he usually does when touring with them.

Stamos took to the mic to say that he knows the UK don't know him as well as the US, but he tours with The Beach Boys whenever he can as he's a huge fan. He said he'd enjoyed an interview with a guy who proposed to his wife using the song "Forever", so he and The Beach Boys sang it and dedicated it to us. It was such a special moment that Lisa and I will cherish "forever".

After the gig, we caught up with Stamos and The Beach Boys, and he

introduced us to them as "his friend". I still say John Stamos is my friend (he said it) and Lisa says he was just polite. We know who's right.

Lisa, me and our friend John Stamos

Hulk Hogan

Although I have never officially met the "Hulkster", I can safely say that I have had enough interactions with him to merit a couple of "clangs".

When I first started doing community radio, a few guys and I created a Wrestling Show where we would talk all about the recent happenings in the world of WWE. Sometimes, we'd secure some pretty cool guests by phone. One of those guests was Eric Bischoff, who was a big name in 1990's wrestling. We had a great interview with him, so much so that he sent me an email a few days later saying how much he enjoyed it and that he would vouch for us any time we wanted to use him as a reference. Now, you know by now that I live by the mantra of "you don't ask, you don't get" and this was no exception. I hit reply to Eric and said: "I know you are close to Hulk Hogan, do you think he would join us for an interview?"

The email trail was quiet for about a week when my phone pinged, and it was Eric. The email read:

"Terry would love to do it, his number is…"

My co-hosts and I were buzzing! We sat in the studio ready to interview the biggest wrestling star ever, and he didn't disappoint. He was everything you'd expect Hulk Hogan to be. He called each of us "brother" as we all stood around the mixing desk chatting to a legend! After that phone call, the atmosphere in the room was electric. Hulk Hogan exudes some amount of energy, and we could feel it even over a phone call. It was awesome! Like the wrestling geek that I am, I kept his number in my phone for those "bragging rights" or "clang" moments. One night I was DJing, and a few drunkards (not friends of mine) got a hold of my phone and ended up looking through the contacts. They came across Hulk Hogan and hit "FaceTime", probably not expecting much. When that trademark bleached blonde moustache and hair person answered and was looking back at them, there was an almighty cheer as they were delighted to see it was him. He changed his number after that, and I don't blame him.

I've met some fascinating people from the Kaiser Chiefs to Mr Tumble; Olly Murs to Eddie the Eagle; Sharleen Spiteri from Texas to Aaron Crascall and Chris Jericho to Grado. The one thing I've learned from meeting every person of influence is that they are as nice to you as you are to them, and they are just humans – just like you and me. Also, mentioning them in a story makes a good "clang" now and then.

10 WEIGHT

Dealing with post-natal Depression and getting up at 4 am for radio had negative consequences for my mental and physical health. It was during this time that my weight started to increase. I used to tell myself when I was at 16-stone I'd sort it out at 17-stone. When I reached 17-stone, that increased to 18-stone. When I hit 18 stone, I told myself not to panic and not to get worried until I hit the 20-stone mark. It got out of control.

Below was a typical day:

4 am – wake up and grab a slice of toast on the way out the door
5 am – visit the shop next to the radio station and buy two butteries (savoury bread rolls), a grab bag of skips, two chocolate bars and two full-fat bottles of cola.
10 am – finish radio show
Noon – leave the station and visit Butties and grab a coronation

chicken baguette, a pie and a can of Irn Bru.

Side note: I mentioned Butties once, while on the radio, saying how lovely their coronation chicken baguettes were and they stopped charging me. It was a very kind gesture but didn't help me combat the eating issue.

1 pm – Arrive home and have lunch with Lisa

I had consumed more than my daily recommended number of calories before lunchtime, and it's clear now that I'd lost control of my food intake.

3 pm – some kind of snack, but limited because Lisa was with me
5 pm – evening meal
9 pm – some sort of snack, or on the odd occasion, order a takeaway for Lisa and me to share

I was getting desperate. My weight was absurd, and I wasn't happy. I tried all sorts of fad diets, meal replacement shakes, slimming clubs and nothing stuck. I'd do well for a couple of weeks (while I still had motivation) and I'd reward my "good results" with a takeaway. This

I topped the scales at 25 stone

reward would become two takeaways, then three in the week and before I knew it, I was back to where I started. At my heaviest, I was 25-stone. Telling someone of this weight, with a food addiction, they just need to "eat less and move more" felt as ridiculous as telling a short person all they had to do to grow taller was to stand in soil. I needed the motivation to last longer than two weeks.

While browsing social media, I came across an ad for an overweight person who wanted to become a wrestler. I thought "oh! This is me!" and contacted the show This Time Next Year. The concept was both complicated and straightforward: you'd walk in and chat with Davina McCall at 25-stone, tell her your goals for "this time next year" and she'd walk you off into another door wishing you well. You'd then enter the stage a year later (seconds later in TV-land), and I appeared as a 16-stone, spandex-clad Chris, otherwise known as "The Commentator".

In real life, it was a year between the 25-stone me, and the 16-stone me, and I spent that year working my butt off! ITV assigned me with a personal trainer who put me through my paces. He was my friend, Russell Fox, and I'd known him for years. I trusted him, and I knew he understood mental ill health, so I felt comfortable with him. He taught me about nutrition and got me into a shape where I was fit enough to train to wrestle.

I contacted the wrestling company I'd commentated for before the show and asked if they'd be interested in helping me achieve my goal. During one of the  storylines, "Felix Fortune" (Callum McMinn) and I had a feud, so they decided to build on this. SWE asked Ian Ambrose (a fantastic wrestling trainer) to help us choreograph a match worth of the build-up and the cameras. Callum and Ian didn't need to do what they did, but they gave their time and skills to help me, and I will be forever grateful to them.

On the night of the match, the ITV cameras arrived early, followed me for interviews, and took shots of the wrestling ring, etc. I was buzzing!

I was ready to get out there and perform – that's what I do! SWE owner announced the match, "Ladies and gentlemen, please welcome to the ring: Chris "The Commentator" Duke." Eye of the Tiger played as I entered the room. Russell was my "manager" for the evening, and it was an honour to have him beside me after training with him for so long. Some signs read "GO CHRIS GO" and "THE COMMENTATOR" and I spotted Lisa, Alyssa and Summer looking up at me. I seized a moment to take it all in. I made my way to the ring after high fiving the spectators, climbed in and amped-up the fans. I relished the moment. The bell rang; it was time to wrestle.

The adrenaline pumping through my veins was enough to make me forget most of the match, and it was over before I realised. There is one part I can't forget. Callum was notorious for being a bit too low on his drop-kick (a kick where you jump in the air and kick the opponent on the chest). The gag was when Callum drop-kicks you, watch your knees! We practised that drop-kick over and over, to the

point where we nailed the height, the reaction and everything else. Well, the adrenaline must have got to him too, as not only did he miss my

Getting my teeth knocked out of my head, and I loved every minute

chest, but he jumped so high that he drop-kicked me to my face! He kicked me square on the chin, clattering my teeth together. Two of my teeth fell out that night, so I literally can't forget that moment – twice a day, for 2 minutes at a time.

A few months after the match, I flew back down to London to record the reveal of me This Time Next Year, and I remember feeling so nervous. It was the same studio that Ant and Dec record Saturday Night Takeaway as well, which felt like a big deal – I'm a fan of them. Davina looked precisely the same as the year previous. Her contract said she couldn't alter her appearance at all, and she had the dress and shoes she wore kept in a specific location so it wouldn't get marked, lost or anything else. She also wasn't allowed to get pregnant during that year, so her body didn't change either. It was an intense year. I'd worked so hard and lost 11 stone. I was fitter, healthier, regularly had the motivation as the camera crew would visit throughout the year for updates, and once we wrapped my segment, the first thing I said was, "Right. Pizza." It wasn't long before I was 25-stone (and everything that came with that) all over again.

I'm a food addict. Food addiction is hard to overcome; we have to eat to survive. I am a forty-cigarettes-a-day ex-smoker. I tried to quit over and over, using all the aids available: gum, patches, willpower, hypnosis, literature and none of them worked. An experimental drug, designed to help people quit smoking, came on the market. It was only available via a GP, and my doctor resisted giving it to me at first.

Eventually, after exhausting all other tools they had, she prescribed me with it, and it was the one that worked. On January 11th, 2010, I smoked my last cigarette. I had finally found the correct tool/aid to help me. My food addiction is no different, in my opinion. I tried all the diets, shakes, etc., and none of them helped me overcome my addiction to food. Food was my downfall. I could exercise as much as I wanted, I enjoy exercising as it is helpful for my mental health, but in terms of weight loss, it doesn't work because I overeat. I decided to approach my food addiction like my smoking addiction and searched for a different aid.

In October 2017, I checked into Nuffield Hospital in Glasgow to prepare for a gastric band operation. Now, let me get this bit out the way because I want to be abundantly clear: gastric bands or any other weight loss surgery is NOT an easy way out. It is a device that HELPS you lose weight by forcing you to reduce the amount of food you can eat. There are forums everywhere with people saying that their gastric band hasn't worked for them, etc. The reason for this, I believe, is because they are waiting for the surgery to do the work for them. It doesn't work like that. You have to work WITH the surgery/device to get the desired results. A gastric band is a device that is clamped around your stomach to give you two pouches. The first pouch is about 20% of the size of your actual stomach, and it fills with food. This restriction tells your brain that you're full and to stop eating. It then trickles down through to your second pouch for digestion. It doesn't suit everyone, but this suited me. It was a strange feeling to go from being able to eat a large pizza on my own to struggling to eat one slice. The feeling of "being full" was foreign to me, and it was a bit daunting at first. It wasn't long, being 25-stone, that the weight started to fall off, and the device started to work.

Christmas, 2018, I stepped onto my scales, and I'd hit that 12.5-stone weight loss marker – my target. That was half my weight gone. I know measuring weight loss on scales aren't everything, and I feel as proud of my NSVs (non-scale victories) as I do my scale ones – probably more. I was able to climb into the loft without worrying the floor would collapse under me, I could fit into a 34-inch waist (56-inch was my largest), I could see my toes, I found clothes at the front of the railing in shops. Still, the most significant difference was that I could now play with my children. When I was 25-stone, I'd tell myself that I was playing with my kids, but realistically, I'd lie on the floor and let them run about me or use me as a climbing frame. At my target weight, I took part in the Dad race at Alyssa's sports day at school; I came last, but the point is I took part. The year before that, I'd have hidden away to avoid any sort of eye-contact with the teachers asking us to join. I could feel the motivation inside me shift when I started to feel healthier. I was lighter: physically and mentally. I felt worthy and set my site on a project that would change my life forever.

11 LUCY

For years I had the line "it's okay, sometimes, to have a blue day" in my head and I knew that I had to do something with this. I had no idea what.

Alyssa had a particularly bad day at school one day, and as I was getting her settled for bed, I decided to stay with her while she drifted off to sleep. After a few minutes of silence, she said, "Daddy, do you ever just not like being you?" This question took my breath away. There had been many a time when I'd been disappointed that I'd woke up the next day after making it through the night, and that type of thought started with me not liking myself. I took a moment, looked at Alyssa and said, "Honey, if you weren't you, you wouldn't be the unique, kind, loving little person you are. I love you very much, just as you are. Why don't you close your eyes and think about how much your daddy loves you?" I kissed her on the forehead and said goodnight. She gave me a tired smile, closed her eyes and drifted off to sleep.

I watched Alyssa sleep, so peacefully. I didn't want my children bottling up their emotions the way I did. I wanted them to know that getting all sort of feelings out was essential. I didn't want my children to go through what I went through. I took my phone out and, anxiously, opened the notes app. I started typing.

"Lucy Pear has wonderful hair; it changes colour like no other."

And before I knew it, there was a poem about a girl with magical colour-changing hair that changed with her emotions; Lucy Pear was born. I couldn't wait for Alyssa to read it, but she'd have to wait until morning; I went into the living room to show Lisa.

"Chris, this is lovely. I mean the grammar is terrible, but I think we should get this illustrated and turned into a little book for the kids."

I thought it was a great idea! It was May, so we thought it would make a lovely birthday or Christmas gift for Alyssa, so we had plenty of time – so we thought. I went to Facebook and asked if anyone I knew had a connection to an illustrator. My old school friend, Joseph Murray, sent me a message about a friend he had from Italy, who was a professional graphic designer. He passed on her information, and we met Federica Bartolini. I'd seen her illustrations on her website and fell in love; I knew she was "the one". Her designs seemed so sweet and honest, but so beautifully intricate at the same time. After an initial conversation, Federica agreed to do it, and she was going to do it free of charge as it was something for our children's mental health – a subject close to her heart. We understood that paid work came first, as it should, but our dreams of this book becoming ready in time got pushed further and further away with paid work taking precedence. I asked Federica for a fee to make it paid work, therefore a priority, and she came back with a figure. First off, I couldn't believe she was willing to do it for free, and secondly, completely understood why paid work took precedence.

It was suggested by someone on social media that we organise a Crowdfund to help pay for Federica's skill. It seemed to be our only option, as money is something we don't have, so I decided to go public with the book idea and set up a page stating that the people who donated a certain amount would receive a copy of a printed book. It did a lot better than I anticipated. We got about 2/3 of the target, and then we hit a wall. Donations started to slow down. I felt like I'd failed because I hadn't hit my target. Then, something incredible happened. I received a notification that Lesley Higgins wanted to send me a message. "Lesley Higgins", I thought..." I know that name." Then I realised we'd been in a musical together a few years before. I opened the message:

"Hi Chris, I'm sure you may be aware of my recent change in circumstance..." and I had absolutely no idea. It then clicked that this was the same Lesley I'd heard around the grapevine who'd won the lottery. She and her husband, Fred, had won £58million in the Euro Millions jackpot, and she wanted to meet with me to discuss what I was doing. I met up with Fred and Lesley a few weeks later, and they were unbelievably generous with what they were saying about what Lisa and I were doing. They agreed to pay the remaining balance of Federica's fee, which was enough! Their generous donation helped get the book finished, and my dream of my little poem becoming a book was possible. Lesley used to work at the local printing company in Forfar, and before I knew it, we were sitting in the boss' office discussing printing bulk copies of my book with Astute Printing. I won't go into details of the amount, but Andrew (the boss) gave us a quote for 5,000 copies of "Lucy's Blue Day", and Lesley said, "Who do I make the cheque out to?" I was stunned. I couldn't believe the kindness of Fred and Lesley, the general public who'd donated to our Crowd Fund, to those who'd supported us from the start, and to every other person who helped make this dream come true. It was very overwhelming. Once it became a tangible book, the pre-orders were starting to come in. It was happening. This little poem was a children's

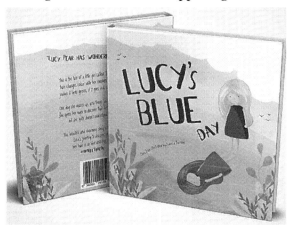

book, and people were buying it for their kids!

"Lucy's Blue Day" was officially released on February 8th, 2018. We held an event at Dundee United Football Club, the local press came along, as did pupils from a few of the schools in the area. It was incredible! They were all here for this book that I'd created. We started receiving feedback too. "The book is beautiful", "the book has helped my little girl" were a lot of the reviews, and then we received the following email:

Good morning,

I just wanted to let you know the impact your book has had on a little boy's life. I am a carer for a little boy who lost his mum last summer, he wouldn't eat, he wouldn't speak, and he wouldn't cry.

Between his mum passing and recently, he had attempted to "go to heaven to be with mummy" a good number of times. We tried everything with him, therapy, every book under the sun and we ordered your book in the hope that it might help. If not, it would just be added to the pile of many books that we bought him to help.

We read the book to him and he looked up, and he smiled for the first time in 8 months. Your book is now part of his treatment, we read it to him twice a day, and he hasn't self-harmed once since we started reading it to him.

Thank you for creating such a wonderful book; you have brought this little boy back.

I can't even begin to describe how I felt reading that email. I showed it to Lisa, and she became overwhelmed too. How do you process that? How do you begin to take responsibility in knowing that something you created has helped save a child's life? Rereading it makes me so emotional.

In March, I was invited to a couple of schools to share my story to talk to the students about how "Lucy's Blue Day" came to be, what it was like to be an author and to share my journey. Other schools heard of my visits, so asked if I'd go to their school as well. Within  a month, Lisa was working from home booking the schools, organising my diary, looking after the kids and keeping the home, and I was travelling hundreds of miles sharing my book with children all over the UK. Life became a whirlwind of mayhem. I felt so happy.

I was no longer feeling disappointed when I woke up. Lucy changed my life. Lucy saved my life.

12 JAMES' STORY

A few years ago, I attended a fundraiser for a group in Sunderland called "Creative Minds". They are a charitable organisation that help children through many different mental health struggles using creative therapy and techniques. It was at this event I met a young man called James. He reminded me of me when I was younger, but with one difference: he already knew that "Big Boys Do Cry".

This is James story:

About three and a half years ago, I started to notice something a little strange. I was scared, a lot, and I didn't know why. The main emotion I felt, at the time, was fear, but I know I had lots of other different feelings too. This was all new to me, and I didn't understand what was going on. Thankfully, my local area has lots of various Mental Health groups, and the best one, in my opinion, is Creative Minds. Nicola, and everyone at Creative Minds, helped me a lot. We had different types of talking sessions: group, one-to-one and relaxing ones and I quickly saw that all different people of ages, from different backgrounds were all going through the same as me. I learned very soon that Mental Illness is nothing to be ashamed of.

Joining Creative Minds changed my life. Not only did I realise that I was going to be ok, but because of how well I responded to the courses and the sessions, Nicola made me an ambassador for Creative Minds. I still attend the sessions, but now I go not only for me but to help other people too. I have been nominated for a "Young Achievers Award" also.

When all this started, I began to develop movements I couldn't control. I knew this wasn't right and asked for help and just a few weeks ago received a diagnosis of Tick Disorder and Obsessive Thought Disorder. It's a huge relief to have this diagnosis now, and it will help me on my road to recovery.

I first met Chris at a fundraiser for Creative Minds, where Nicola invited Chris as a guest. Chris is kind and helped me a lot with his books. Whenever I feel sad, I think about "Lucy's Blue Day", and it puts a smile on my face. Chris' books make me happy. The one message in the book has stayed with me throughout, and it is this:

It's ok to feel angry;
It's ok to feel mad;
It's ok to feel happy;

It's ok to feel sad.

It'll be alright, I know.

When deciding on what to put on the cover of this book, I didn't need to think twice when James came to mind. He is a kind, considerate and resilient lad who will do so well in life. James is an absolute legend and I am glad to know him.

TECHNIQUES

Disclaimer: These techniques are practices I've picked up over the years that have helped me. I am not medically trained; neither is Lisa, but we felt these were worth sharing.

The Picture Frame Technique

Everything I've overcome in terms of my self-sabotage and anxieties is a work-in-progress, and probably always will be. I didn't wake up one morning and feel like I could take on the world and feel confident in myself – as good as that would have been. I do different things depending on each situation where I find myself struggling.

The way I deal with stressful situations or anxious thoughts is called The Picture Frame Technique. I was taught this by Tony Lawson, who is a life coach at Tony Lawson Coaching. Before trying this, I'd advise you read the whole process as it will involve closing your eyes – it's harder to read like that.

Step 1: Imagine that stressful situation.
My marriage is falling apart.

Step 2: Imagine the worst-case scenario in this situation.
Lisa is packing her bags and taking the kids with her.

Step 3: Take this scenario and take a snapshot of it in your mind.
Lisa is standing at the door with suitcases and the kids holding her hands.

Step 4: Thinking of this snapshot think about how anxious this image makes you feel on a scale of 1 to 10.
10

Step 5: Take the image and put a frame around it. Take the colour out the picture, so it's now in black and white. Where is it on the scale now?
8

Step 6: Take the black and white image and move it over to the corner of the room, until all you can see is a tiny square. Where is it on the scale now?
2

The point of this exercise is to help take the stress out of a situation, and to help you think clearly on it. Lisa and I have gone through so much together (more than I've written) and I'm very grateful that despite it all, she stayed with me. We've been working hard on our relationship ever since. I've accepted that if she decides to leave, there's nothing I can do about it. Using the picture frame technique, you are distancing yourself from the worst-case scenario, and you can move forward in a way that you can control.

Feed Your Butterfly

This technique I tell children about when I tour the schools talking about Lucy's Blue Day, emotions and my journey.

Think about something that makes you feel really happy – that kind of "happy" that makes you smile.

A lot of the children in the schools go for ice-cream, hugs, Christmas and so on, and they're perfect for younger people. Mine is my girls.

I ask them to note the feeling in their tummy; it's like butterflies.

This butterfly doesn't eat typical food; it eats special food called Happy Thoughts. I am the only person who can feed my butterfly. If I feel down one day, I think of all the things that make me feel happy; those things that make my butterfly dance about inside my tummy. I keep thinking about them until I feel better.

This technique can help a child feel a little better and brings them to an emotional state where they can talk about what got them feeling sad in the first place. It's also an excellent way to introduce gratitude: think of 5 things that make you feel happy. It allows the person to focus on the good things in their life, especially if they're feeling a little low from what life throws at them.

When I do my school sessions, I run through a 4-part checklist with the students. I say there are four things I wanted to be when I grow up:

1.   A dad
2.   A DJ
3.   An author
4.   A wrestler

And I go on to tell the students my journey (a lot shorter than this book and kid-friendly). I explain that the secret to my success in achieving these goals is nothing more than determination; never giving up.

When I became a dad, I was diagnosed with post-natal-Depression. It would have been easy for me to give up. I could have walked away or done something worse. I didn't, thankfully. I fought through with the incredible support of my wife, and we have the most amazing family. When I wanted to be a DJ, I phoned Wave 102 every day for a year before they let me through the doors. I could have given up after the first unreturned call, but I didn't. I ended up achieving another goal and got to be a radio DJ. When I weighed 25-stone and the opportunity to wrestle presented itself to me, I could have given up. I could have quit when it got challenging, but I didn't. I kept going, and I got to live that dream. Becoming an author, even by accident, was achieved because I didn't give up on the idea to make my poem into a book. I could have given up when we hit the first financial hurdle, or when we got told our book was offensive to red-heads (as a red-head, with a red-headed child, and red-headed nieces and nephews; this is nonsense) but I didn't.

I make a promise with the students I go and see, and I'm going to make that promise with you too. I would also like you to make a promise to me before the end of this book. I promise that no matter what age you are, no matter what obstacles are in your way, whatever you want to achieve in your life, you can do so long as you don't give up! Come and find me in a year and tell me a goal that you've set yourself right now. Let me know whether you've achieved it or not, and if you have, amazing! Let me know all about it. If you haven't yet, I will ask you one question: "Have you given up?" If the answer is yes, I'll tell you to keep going.

Now, the promise I'd like you to make to me is called The Lucy

Promise. It's what the students promise me at the end of each of my school sessions, and I'd love for you to take part:

Stand up. Seriously, stand up.

Raise your right hand while holding the book open at this page (if you can) and say the following:

"I (say your name) promise: if I feel angry, jealous, sad or happy, I will tell someone because, it's okay to feel angry, it's okay to feel jealous, it's okay to feel sad, and it's okay to feel happy!"

The Magic Hand Technique

Another great one for children.

You take your pointer finger from one hand and place it on the outside of your thumb on the other hand. As you inhale through your nose, slowly glide your finger up your thumb.

As you slowly slide down the other side of your thumb, exhale out your mouth.

Repeat this process on each finger: inhale through the nose, exhale out the mouth until you reach the pinkie.

If the child is still in their heightened state of emotion, they can start from the pinkie and go back to the thumb.

Repeat as necessary until the child is back in control of the situation, and you can talk to them about how they're feeling – when they're ready.

Lisa is adding a technique she uses that has helped her be a lot kinder to herself, especially as a working mum.

The Kindness Mirror

I hope you don't mind me jumping in here, but I wanted to share this technique as it has helped me overcome mum guilt, the feeling of having to be perfect, have everything done and still have enough energy to be the best mum/wife/daughter, etc.

I'd like you to close your eyes or find a picture in your house or phone of the person/people you cherish most in the world. Take the time to paint a clear image in your mind; if you have a video of them, even better! Watch it and just take in the feelings you feel when you do.

Now think about yourself. How has your mood changed? How have your feelings changed? Now, ask yourself: would you wish those people you love and treasure to ever feel about themselves the way you think about yourself? If you feel good about yourself, this is truly wonderful! I hope you teach those people to love themselves the same way you love you.

If you don't, don't worry. Don't be too hard on yourself; you've not done anything wrong. You've just forgotten to value yourself as worthy, and through time, patience and compassion, your value will improve.

Take at least 20 minutes a week (start with 5 minutes if needed) where you do something that's for you.

My favourite things to do is to: sit with a hot cup of tea and drink it from start to end without speaking to anyone; sit in silence for 15 minutes and watch the trees around me; take my dogs a walk where I can let them run off the lead, and I can be present in that moment; sit on a park bench and watch as parts of the world go by; give myself a break WHEN I make mistakes; apologise and forgive myself for losing my temper, and letting it go; thanking my body growing three exceptional humans, feeding them and being healthy.

As a mum, there is still a societal "obligation" to be perfect, organised and brilliant all the time, and I'm here to tell you that it is NOT possible. Something has to give, and I think one of the first things to go should be the pressure we put on ourselves to do it all and to do it all flawlessly!

I've called this The Kindness Mirror Technique because we need to reflect a lot of the kindness and compassion that we show others to ourselves.

Personify Depression

You may have noticed that the word "Depression" starts with a capital D in this book. The reason for this is because it's the piece of advice I received when asking for help on how to support someone who suffers. I am fortunate not to experience Depression the way many people have, and I thank Chris and those who are open and honest about it helps people like me understand. Without your strength, we can't sympathise.

I was a member of a baby forum, and I asked for help on how to best support Chris with his mental illness. I can't remember the name of the person who said it, but she said to personify Depression – turn it into a third entity in your relationship. It's not helpful at all; it will do everything it can to get in the way and destroy the sufferer's happiness, and if it can bring you down too, all the better as far as Depression is concerned.

It was a definite turning point in helping me understand it. I stopped putting all the blame on Chris for things he'd do. I wasn't naïve enough to think that he was at no fault, but it helped me understand that it wasn't Chris who was lying in bed for days on end, unable to get up; it was his Depression telling him not to bother. It was his Depression telling him he wasn't good enough, just as he is. It was Depression that would make him feel inadequate as a dad and a husband, so it helped me realise there was a lot more to it than him just acting like a lazy idiot, which is what I thought.

I have to help him fight it. He has to want to, but Chris has to know he's not alone and I will do everything I can to make sure of that. It's not easy, and mistakes happen, but when communication is open and acknowledged, I promise you it will make a massive difference.

FINAL THOUGHTS

The only person standing in your way is you. Me vs Me was the original name of this book because I realised the only person standing in my way to achieving my goals was me. No one made me self-harm; I did that. No one made me put that nail on Lindsay McLean's chair; it was me. No one made me lie to my best friend to impress him; no one forced me to eat 5,000 calories a day; no one made me lie to my parents, my wife, myself – all me! Similarly, no one made me learn those three chords to sing with Mel C; no one made me entertain 10,000 members of the public at that concert, and no one forced me to train and achieve my dream of having a wrestling match – also, all me!

YOU are the master of YOUR destiny. No one else is going to make it happen. I have to tell myself this every single day, so start telling yourself this too.

I wanted to write this book to help adults understand that they're not alone in what they go through. Those of us who are over-thinkers; believe me when I say there are millions of us, our negative thoughts like to tell us we're on our own, unworthy, bothersome, and so on and trust me, it's all false. I didn't intend on this becoming an autobiography, but it's sort of morphed into that as time has gone on, and I want to give my heartfelt thanks for taking the time to read it.

To my mum and dad – I'm so sorry for every single lie I've told you. I'm sorry for the stress I put you through when I buggered off to Germany without notifying you. I'm sorry for causing you so much stress and worry that you lay awake at night wondering what I'd do next, and I'm sorry that, through my selfish behaviours, I almost cost you your grandchildren.

To unnamed friends – I have sabotaged many friendships throughout my life because of my anxiety. I haven't mentioned these moments because I don't think the people in question would like it brought to light. I just want to apologise for being so paranoid at times that I created scenarios where I thought you were trying to sabotage me when I was doing a fine job of it myself. I'm sorry for the unnecessary stress you went through because of me.

Although it's nice to get the negatives "out there", it's more important to focus on the positives. I wouldn't be anywhere near the person I am without the support and encouragement from friends and family;

I wouldn't be alive today if it weren't for some of them.

Mum and Dad - thank you for your support, your unconditional love, even when I didn't deserve it, and thank you for being brilliant grandparents to our children.

To my in-laws – I know I haven't always been the ideal partner you'd want for your daughter. Still, I hope to improve continually and thank you for always being supportive of me and also being incredible grandparents to our children.

I don't have many friends as I prefer quality over quantity, but the friends that I do have are very, very special to me. Brian means the world to me, but I have to mention a few more. Colin, one of my closest friends, is a guy who always helps you if he can – and he usually can. Colin is more family than a friend to Lisa and me, and we love him dearly. Grant Roach is a man who I clicked with right away. No matter what, he just gets me, and I feel like I get him. Lisa calls Grant "my other spouse" and it's not far off the truth. We are very similar, with similar interests, and he will always be the person who introduced me to Hamilton.

To my wife, my rock and my love. None of this would be here if it wasn't for you, I wouldn't be here if it wasn't for you. You have changed and saved my life in more ways than you will ever know and I will spend my days letting you know and showing you how much I appreciate every single thing you do for me and our family. I said earlier that "Lucy saved my life" but there is another life saver out there too, and her name also begins with L and has 4 letters.

"Look around at how lucky we are to be alive right now."

ABOUT THE AUTHOR

Chris Duke is a former radio presenter, party DJ and father-of-three who has suffered from mental health issues throughout his life. He went through a particularly dark patch of depression after the birth of his first daughter in 2010. He realised he wasn't feeling "quite right" when the Health Visitor did the post-partum questionnaire with his wife, Lisa. She suggested that Chris should answer the questions and the Health Visitor then suggested he seek medical help and advice as based on the questionnaire results he was suffering from post-natal depression.

Chris then spent some time fighting for Dads to be offered the questionnaire as well as the Mums – after all, they become a parent too! He then realised that the stigma associated with mental health is taught throughout life. We could teach kids to break that stigma by educating them on thoughts and feelings and encouraging them to open up without fear of shame from a young age. This is when Chris decided to take his book idea public.

Chris has no qualifications regarding mental health issues other than his own experiences, nevertheless, this has not stopped him hitting the mark for helping children express their thoughts and feelings and "Lucy's Blue Day" is making strides in achieving his ultimate goal: to teach kids that #ItsOKNotToBeOK and to open up about their feelings.

Printed in Poland
by Amazon Fulfillment
Poland Sp. z o.o., Wrocław

65234360R00089